Celebrate Reading

Written by
Maureen McCourt Boylan
and
Traci Ferguson Geiser, M.A.

Editor: Collene Dobelmann
Illustrator: Darcy Tom
Designer/Production: Moonhee Pak/Carrie Rickmond
Cover Designer: Moonhee Pak
Art Director: Tom Cochrane
Project Director: Carolea Williams

Table of Contents

Introduction

Need a reason to celebrate? *Celebrate Reading* gives you twelve. This reproducible collection of leveled, high-interest stories written specifically for emergent and early fluency readers draws on the traditions and customs of twelve different cultural celebrations to help children learn to read.* The coordinating lessons and cross-curricular activities show you how to use these reproducible stories to teach the five key areas of reading instruction—phonemic awareness, phonics, fluency, vocabulary, and comprehension.

Interesting and developmentally appropriate text makes each reproducible story the perfect tool for guided and independent reading. Clear activity directions explain how children can expand phonemic awareness, mark up their reproducibles to reinforce phonics lessons, improve fluency, develop vocabulary, and facilitate text comprehension during both small-group and whole-class instruction. The reproducible pages are also convenient for children to take home and read to a friend or family member. Additional interactive lessons, which are directly linked to the text of each story, target the key areas of reading instruction and make this resource the perfect complement to your regular literacy program.

Children love to celebrate the holidays. Lead them through the activities in *Celebrate Reading*, and they can celebrate their success with reading throughout the school year!

*These stories are also available as individual full-color books (16 pages each) in Creative Teaching Press's *Learn to Read Holiday Series*.

How to Use This Book

Simply photocopy class sets of the story at the beginning of each section, and read the story to children. Encourage them to follow the text with their fingers as you read. Discuss the story with children.

Have children refer to their reproducible stories as you lead them through the Instant Lessons. Coaching children in the five key areas of reading instruction will facilitate real progress. Activities involving these areas of instruction are designated on the Instant Lessons pages by the icons listed below:

 *Phonemic Awareness* concentrates on the sound units (phonemes) used to form spoken words. It helps children learn to read and spell new words.

 *Phonics* helps children associate sounds with written symbols (i.e., the alphabet). It improves word recognition, spelling, and comprehension.

 *Fluency* is the ability to read text with ease. A fluent reader automatically recognizes words and thereby reads quickly, confidently, and with the freedom to concentrate on comprehension.

 *Vocabulary* includes the words we use to communicate. A good reader understands the meaning of words encountered in print.

 *Comprehension* is an understanding of what is being read. An active reader uses reading strategies and knowledge about language and the world to understand and discuss text.

Invite children to participate in interactive literacy, writing, math, and art activities designed to extend learning and help them develop an appreciation for the holiday they are celebrating. Activities marked with a Seasons Stamp icon are ideal center activities but can easily be adapted for whole-group instruction.

Have fun. Learning to read is a great reason to celebrate!

The Pilgrims sailed to America.
They were thankful for their new home.
I am thankful for my new home.

The Pilgrims came to America to be free.
They were thankful for their freedom.
I am thankful for my freedom.

The Pilgrims wanted to learn about the world.
They were thankful for their schools.
I am thankful for my school.

The Pilgrims met new people in America.
They were thankful for their new friends.
I am thankful for my new friends.

The Pilgrims had a hard winter.
They were thankful for people who
     helped them.
I am thankful for people who help me.

The Pilgrims' families worked together.
They were thankful for their families.
I am thankful for my family.

On the first Thanksgiving, the Pilgrims
     were thankful for their feast.
This Thanksgiving, **I am thankful for
     my feast.**
And I am thankful for the Pilgrims.

Instant Lessons

Phonemic Awareness

Identifying Phonemes

Invite children to listen to some words from the reproducible story. Say *home*, *freedom*, and *am*. Then ask children to identify the sound that occurs in all three (i.e., /m/). Repeat this exercise with other groups of words from the story, such as *the*, *they*, *their*; *free*, *feast*, *friends*; *met*, *help*, *them*; and *had*, *am*, *family*. To extend learning, have children identify where the target sound occurs in the word—at the beginning, middle, or end.

Phonics

Consonant Digraph *th*

Ask children to locate and underline on their reproducible story all of the words that begin with *th* (e.g., *thanks*, *the*, *they*, *thankful*, *their*, *Thanksgiving*). Invite children to write other words that begin with *th* on a piece of paper.

Fluency

Partner Reading

Pair fluent readers with nonfluent readers, and ask the fluent reader to read aloud the first section of text. Invite his or her partner to read the same text. Tell children to repeat the process to read the remaining text on the page. Then have both children read aloud the entire page together. Encourage children to assist each other when necessary.

Vocabulary

Using Word Parts

Remind children to use words they know to decipher unfamiliar words. Write *thank* on the board, and invite children to name words that have *thank* in them (e.g., *thanks*, *thankful*, *Thanksgiving*, *thankless*, *thankfulness*, *thankfully*, *thank you*). As you write each new word, emphasize the word *thank*. After the list is complete, have children define each word.

Comprehension

Generating Questions

Invite children to reread their reproducible story several times, and then have them write three questions about the story. Ask children to choose a partner and exchange questions with him or her. Tell children to write the answers to the questions on a separate piece of paper. Have partners use the text to verify that the answers to their questions are correct.

Turkey Tally

SKILL: COUNTING SYLLABLES

Materials

- Turkeys reproducible (page 10)
- Feathers reproducible (page 11)
- crayons or markers
- scissors

Copy, color, and cut apart the Turkeys and Feathers reproducible pages. For a self-checking feature, write on the back of each "feather" the number of syllables the word contains. Place all the cutouts at a center. Arrange the "turkeys" in numerical order on a flat surface. Invite children to read the words on each feather. Tell children to clap and count the syllables they hear in each word and to place the feather on the turkey with the same number. After children have placed all of the feathers, encourage them to reread the words on each turkey. Have children turn over the feathers to check their work.

Scrumptious Pumpkins

SKILL: WRITING STEPS IN A PROCESS

Materials

- Scrumptious Pumpkins reproducible (page 12)
- Recipe Card reproducible (page 13)
- crayons or markers

Copy one Scrumptious Pumpkins reproducible and a class set of the Recipe Card reproducible. Place the pages at a center. Review with children the parts of a recipe. Discuss the importance of including ingredients, oven temperature, baking time, and directions for preparing the recipe. Ask children to choose a recipe from the Scrumptious Pumpkins reproducible, and invite them to write that recipe on a Recipe Card reproducible. Encourage children to take home their recipe card and make the recipe with their family.

Dinner Dollars

SKILLS: COUNTING MONEY AND WRITING A PARAGRAPH

Materials

- Menu Cards reproducible (page 14)
- Dinner Decisions reproducible (page 15)
- scissors

Copy a class set of the Menu Cards and Dinner Decisions reproducible pages. Ask children to cut apart the Menu Cards. Invite children to "shop" for a balanced meal to serve their family for a Thanksgiving celebration. Read with children the price on each Menu Card. Tell children to pretend they have $10 to spend. Give children the Dinner Decisions reproducible, and explain that it will help them keep track of what they buy so they don't overspend. Invite children to select foods from the cards and record them on the planning spaces of the paper. Encourage children to use both "Plan A" and "Plan B" to plan different meal options. Ask them to imagine serving the meal to their family. Then have them write about what might happen at dinner.

corn on the cob $0.50

turkey $4.00

Fancy Feathers

SKILLS: DEVELOPING FINE MOTOR SKILLS AND FOLLOWING DIRECTIONS

Materials

- paintbrushes
- tempera paint (brown, red, orange, yellow)
- 9" x 12" (23 cm x 30.5 cm) white construction paper

Paint the palm and thumb of children's hands with brown paint. Paint the remaining fingers with yellow at the top, orange in the middle, and red at the bottom. Ask children to press their hand down on a piece of white paper. Tell children to hold their thumb and palm in place as they gently move their remaining four fingers from side-to-side (like windshield wipers) to create "feathers." Encourage children to paint eyes, feet, a beak, and a wattle on their turkey.

Turkeys

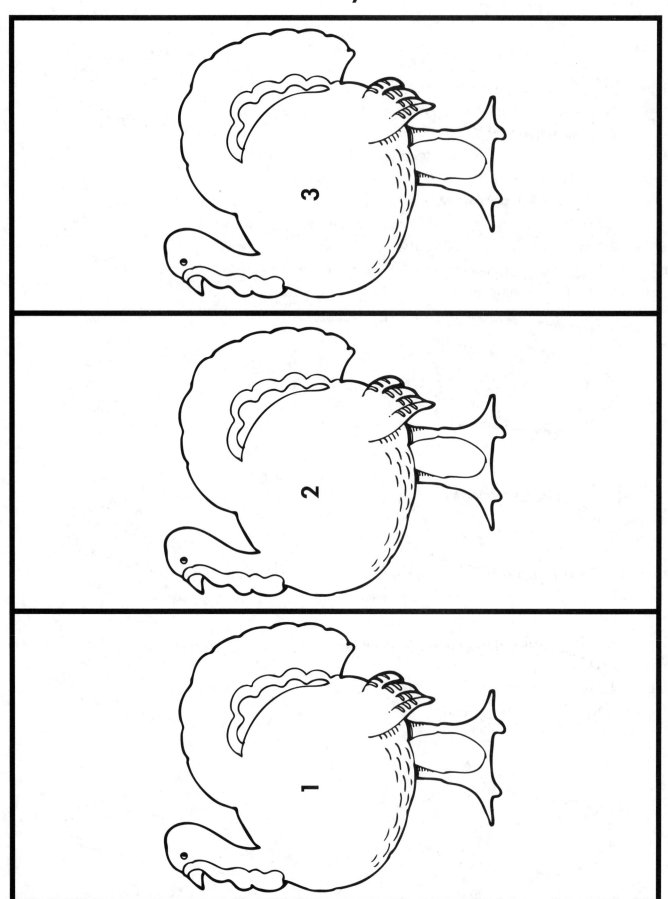

Feathers

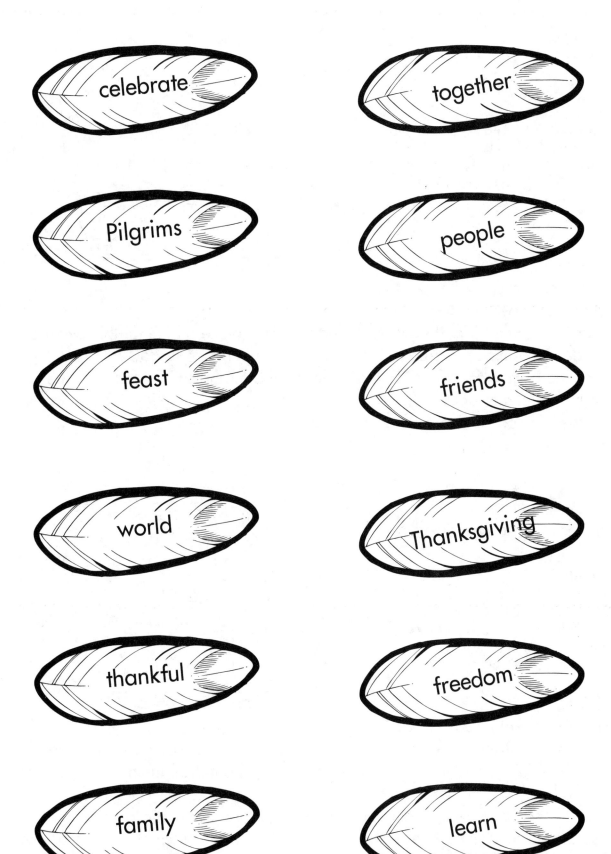

celebrate

together

Pilgrims

people

feast

friends

world

Thanksgiving

thankful

freedom

family

learn

Scrumptious Pumpkins

Perfect Pumpkin Pie

Ingredients:
¾ cup (177 mL) sugar
1½ teaspoons (7.5 mL) pumpkin pie spice
½ teaspoon (2.5 mL) salt
15 ounces (425 g) canned pumpkin
1¼ cups (296 mL) evaporated milk
2 eggs, beaten
1 frozen deep-dish piecrust

Directions:
1. Preheat oven to 425°F (218°C).
2. In a large bowl, stir together the filling ingredients.
3. Pour the mixture into the piecrust, and carefully place on the middle oven rack.
4. Bake for 15 minutes. Then reduce the oven temperature to 350°F (177°C), and continue baking for 40 to 50 minutes or until a toothpick inserted near the center of the pie comes out clean.
5. Let the pie cool. Refrigerate until served.

Roasted Pumpkin Seeds

Ingredients:
1 quart (0.95 L) water
2 tablespoons (30 mL) salt
2 cups (roughly 475 mL) pumpkin seeds
1 teaspoon (5 mL) paprika
1 tablespoon (15 mL) butter

Directions:
1. Preheat oven to 300°F (149°C).
2. Remove the stringy fibers from the seeds, and run cold water over the seeds.
3. Bring the salt and water to a boil. Add the seeds and boil them for 10 minutes.
4. Drain the seeds and let them dry.
5. Pour the seeds in a bowl with melted butter and paprika. Stir to coat.
6. Spread the seeds on a cookie sheet and roast for 35 minutes, stirring occasionally. The seeds are done when they are golden and crispy.

Recipe Card

From the kitchen of _____

Recipe for _____

Ingredients:

_____

_____

_____

_____

_____

Directions:

_____

_____

_____

_____

_____

_____

_____

_____

Menu Cards

mashed potatoes $1.00

ham $4.00

fried chicken $4.00

turkey $4.00

green beans $0.50

spice cake $3.00

pumpkin pie $3.00

corn on the cob $0.50

sweet peas $0.50

rolls $2.00

yams $1.00

squash $1.00

cranberry dessert $2.00

stuffing $3.00

noodle salad $2.00

Name: _____

Dinner Decisions

Plan A

Food	Price
_____	_____
_____	_____
_____	_____
_____	_____
_____	_____

Total: _____

Plan B

Food	Price
_____	_____
_____	_____
_____	_____
_____	_____
_____	_____

Total: _____

_____

_____

_____

_____

_____

On the first night of Chanukah, our family uses the shamash candle from the middle of the menorah to light one candle. Our uncle tells us the Chanukah story.

On the second night of Chanukah, our family lights two candles on the menorah. Our aunt makes potato pancakes. We call them latkes.

On the third night of Chanukah, our family lights three candles on the menorah. We play a game with a top. We call the top a dreidel.

On the fourth night of Chanukah, our family lights four candles on the menorah. We sing songs together.

On the fifth night of Chanukah, our family lights five candles on the menorah. We have a big feast.

On the sixth night of Chanukah, our family lights six candles on the menorah. We get bags full of chocolate coins. We call the coins Chanukah gelt.

On the seventh night of Chanukah, our family lights seven candles on the menorah. We go to our grandmother's house for dinner. We call her Bubbie.

The eighth night of Chanukah is the last night. Our family lights all the candles on the menorah!

Instant Lessons

Phonemic Awareness

Isolating Phonemes

Invite children to listen to the beginning sounds of the words *candle*, *light*, and *coin*. Then ask children which word has a different beginning sound. Repeat with *middle*, *family*, and *menorah*. Follow the same steps to have children identify words with a different middle sound (e.g., *game*, *play*, *songs*; and *get*, *gelt*, *big*) and a different ending sound (e.g., *on*, *feast*, *last*; and *sing*, *five*, *have*).

Phonics

Listening for /īt/

Say *kite*, *fight*, and *write*. Ask children to determine the sound that is similar in each word. Have children underline on their reproducible story all the words that end with that sound. Then draw two columns on a piece of chart paper. Explain to children that /īt/ can be spelled two ways. Spell aloud *-ight* as you write it at the top of the first column, and spell aloud *-ite* as you write it above the second column. Ask children how their underlined words are spelled, and write them in the appropriate column. Have children brainstorm other words that have the same sound at the end, such as *bite*, *kite*, and *bright*. Write the words in the proper column as children think of them.

Fluency

Reader's Theater

Invite children to use the text from their reproducible story as a script. Divide the class into small groups to rehearse their play. Explain to children that the only words they may say are those from the text and that each child must have at least one speaking part. Encourage children to examine the illustrations and reread the text for ideas about how to act out their play. Invite groups to perform their play for each other or another class.

Vocabulary

Using Picture Clues Prior to Reading

Ask children to look at the illustrations on their reproducible story. Have children point to the pictures as you describe *shamash*, *menorah*, *dreidel*, and *Chanukah gelt*. Invite children who are familiar with the items to tell about them. Then have children circle the vocabulary words in the text. Encourage children to use the unfamiliar words when they talk about the story.

Comprehension

Answering Questions

Invite children to look on their reproducible story to find answers as you ask the following questions: *Where is the shamash found on the menorah? What are the potato pancakes that are served during Chanukah called? What is the name for the top that is used in a Chanukah game? How many nights are in a Chanukah celebration? What are the Chanukah gelt coins made of?* Invite children to write their answers on a piece of paper and to exchange papers to check their work.

Menorah Numbers

SKILL: RECOGNIZING ORDINAL NUMBERS

Materials

- Menorah Cards reproducible (page 20)
- Ordinal-Word Cards reproducible (page 21)
- scissors

Copy and cut apart a set of Menorah Cards and Ordinal-Word Cards, and place them at a center. For a self-checking feature, write the corresponding ordinal word on the back of each Menorah Card. Invite children to arrange the Ordinal-Word Cards in numerical order from first to eighth. Tell children to look at the number of candles on the Menorah Cards, and have them match the Menorah Cards with the corresponding Ordinal-Word Cards. (Remind students not to include the shamash candle when counting the candles on the Menorah Cards.) Have children turn over the cards to check their work.

first

Terrific Tops

SKILL: WRITING DESCRIPTIONS

Materials

- Dreidel Game Ad reproducible (page 22)
- newspaper and magazine advertisements
- crayons or markers

Copy a class set of the Dreidel Game Ad reproducible. Show children advertisements, and discuss how they feature pictures and words to sell a product. Invite children to write an ad for a dreidel. Brainstorm with children words that might describe the game. Give children a Dreidel Game Ad reproducible, and tell them to draw a dreidel at the top. Encourage children to write descriptive words, sentences, or paragraphs that might convince others to purchase their Chanukah top.

Dazzling Dreidels

SKILLS: DEVELOPING FINE MOTOR SKILLS AND FOLLOWING DIRECTIONS

Materials

- Dreidel reproducible (page 23)
- scissors
- crayons or markers
- glitter
- glue
- pencils

Copy a class set of the Dreidel reproducible. Have children cut them out along the bolded lines. Encourage children to decorate their dreidel with crayons, markers, or glitter. Help children cut out the circles in their pattern. Then have them fold along the bolded lines and glue together the tabs to make a top. Have children insert a pencil through the holes, and show them how to spin the dreidel. Invite children to use their dreidel at the Spin and Score math center (see below).

Spin and Score

SKILLS: ADDING AND SUBTRACTING

Materials

- Dreidel Tally reproducible (page 24)
- dreidels (real ones or those made in Dazzling Dreidels activity)
- 10–20 counters (e.g., small candies, pennies, or dried beans)

Make a class set of the Dreidel Tally reproducible, and place it at the center. Also place at the center a dreidel and 10 to 20 counters. Invite groups of three to the center at one time. Explain to children what the symbols on the sides of the dreidel mean (see Dreidel Tally reproducible). Invite children to take turns spinning the dreidel and taking or replacing counters as directed. Tell children to use the Dreidel Tally reproducible to record their additions and subtractions. Explain to children that the player who accumulates all of the counters wins.

Menorah Cards

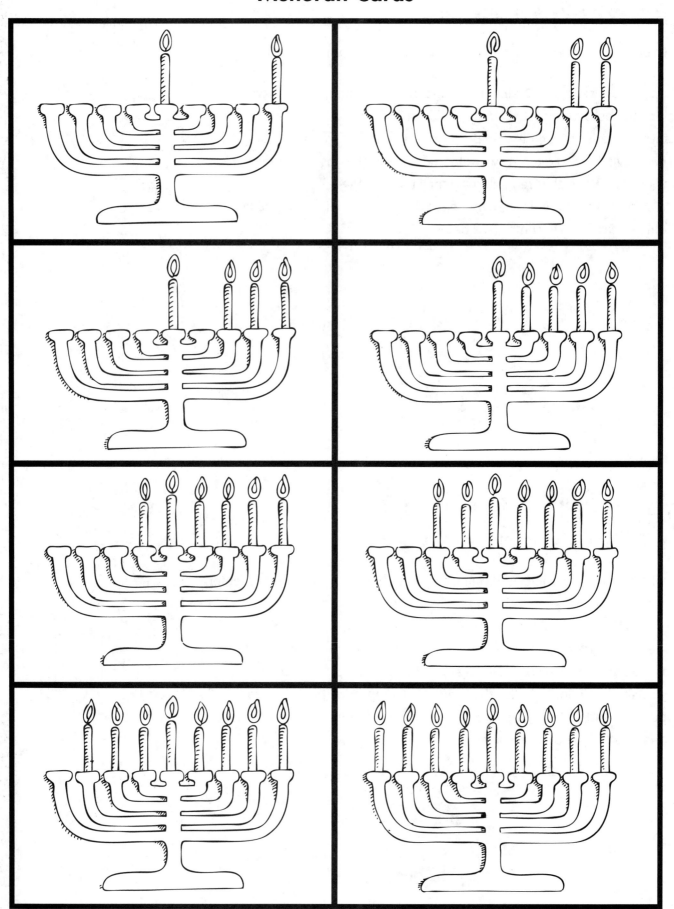

first	second
third	fourth
fifth	sixth
seventh	eighth

Dreidel Game Ad

_____

_____

_____

_____

_____

_____

Dreidel

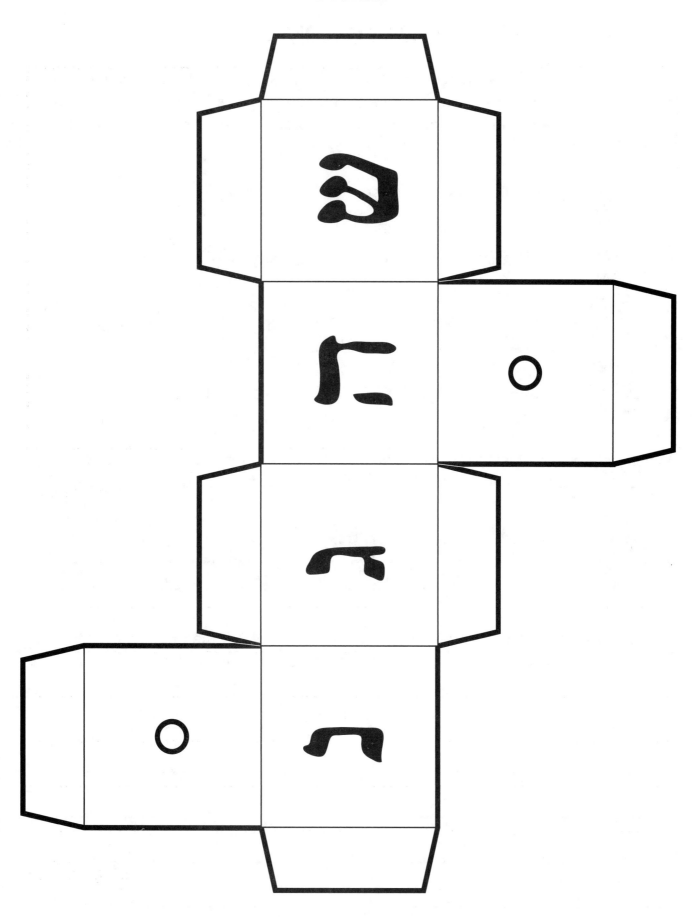

Name: _____

Dreidel Tally

Each player should have an equal number of objects (10 to 20) for counting. Every player places a counter in a center pile. Then each player takes a turn at spinning the dreidel. The letter the dreidel shows when it stops spinning determines what each player should do.

N—Nun stands for "nothing." Do nothing.

G—Gimel stands for "all." Take everything in the middle.

H—Hay stands for "half." Take half of what is in the middle and one more if there is an odd number.

SH—Shin stands for "put in." Put two counters in the center pile.

When only one counter or no counters are left in the center pile, each player must add one. The player who collects all the counters wins the game.

In the top space, write the number of counters you have at the beginning of the game. To keep track of your score, add or subtract from this number each time you take a turn.

_____   _____

_____   _____

_____   _____

_____   _____

Celebrate Reading © 2005 Creative Teaching Press

My family celebrates Christmas. One of the things I like most about Christmas is decorating the house. There is a reason for each decoration.

We set up a nativity scene on our table. It **reminds** us of the manger where the story of Christmas tells us Jesus was born.

Our Christmas tree is a pine tree. We hang candy canes on the tree. The candy canes are shaped like a shepherd's staff to **remind** us of the shepherds who first heard about baby Jesus.

Many of our decorations have angels on them. They **remind** us of the angels who told the shepherds where to find baby Jesus.

We hang a star at the top of the tree. It **reminds** us of the star that led the wise men to baby Jesus.

We put our gifts under the tree. The gifts **remind** us of the gifts the wise men brought to baby Jesus.

When we are finished, the whole house is beautiful. It tells a beautiful story, too! What stories do your holiday decorations tell?

Instant Lessons

Phonemic Awareness

Identifying Phonemes

Invite children to listen to the beginning sound of *Christmas*, *candy*, and *canes*. Ask which sound occurs in all three. Have children identify the common sound in other sets of words, such as *house*, *hang*, *heard*; and *like*, *remind*, *wise*.

Phonics

Short *a* and Long *a* Vowel Sounds

Tell children to listen for the short a sound, and say *family* and *candy*. Invite children to name other words with the short a sound. Read the reproducible story with children, and have them circle words with the short *a* sound. As children identify and circle each word, write it on chart paper, and say it aloud. Then tell children to listen for the long a sound. Say *table* and *cane*, and repeat the previous steps. Review the words with children, and use a yellow marker to highlight the letter or letters that represent the short or long a sound.

Fluency

Partner Reading

Invite parent volunteers or children from higher grade levels to read the reproducible story with children. Pair each child with an adult or older student, and ask the experienced reader to read aloud the reproducible story. Then ask the child to read the story, and encourage the adult or older student to assist when necessary. Invite children to reread the story several times until they are able to read it fluently.

Vocabulary

Defining Words Prior to Reading

Write *remind* on the board. Ask children to think about what they know about the story to help them determine what the word means. Invite children to share their ideas, and then write the definition for *remind* on the board. Ask volunteers to use *remind* in a spoken sentence. Repeat with *manger* and *wise*.

Comprehension

Creating a Chart

Draw a line down the center of a piece of chart paper. Write *Decorations* at the top of the left-hand column and *Reminds people of . . .* at the top of the right-hand column. Invite children to look at their reproducible story and name the decorations they see. Write their observations and review each decoration. Ask children to describe what it reminds the family of, and record their ideas. Encourage children to name other Christmas decorations and what the decorations may remind people of.

Decoration Celebration

SKILL: IDENTIFYING WORDS THAT END IN -TION

Materials

- Nativity reproducible (page 29)
- Stable reproducible (page 30)
- Celebrating Christmas: Christmas Decorations reproducible (page 25)
- crayons or markers
- scissors
- glue
- handwriting paper
- 12" x 18" (30.5 cm x 46 cm) construction paper

Copy class sets of the Nativity and Stable reproducible pages. Read the Celebrating Christmas: Christmas Decorations reproducible with children, and have them find and circle the word *decoration*. Emphasize the ending -*tion*. Read with children the words on the Nativity reproducible, and then define them. To help children identify the images that belong in a nativity

scene, tell them to color and cut out only the pieces from the page that have the -*tion* ending. Then ask children to arrange the pieces on the Stable reproducible to create a nativity scene. Invite children to glue the pieces in place, and then have them color their scene. Have children write on handwriting paper at least three sentences that use the -*tion* words from the nativity scene. Ask children to glue their scene and sentences to construction paper.

Waiting for Christmas

SKILL: USING A CALENDAR

Materials

- December reproducible (page 31)
- crayons or markers

Copy a class set of the December reproducible. Help children number the days of the month on the calendar. Ask them to label special days such as Christmas Day, Christmas Eve, and the first day of Christmas vacation. Have them draw symbols like wreaths or candy canes on those days to denote their importance. Identify what day it is, and ask children questions like

How many weeks (or days) until Christmas Day? How many weeks (or days) until Christmas vacation starts? Have children keep their calendars at their desks, and at the end of each school day, encourage children to mark through the calendar space that represents that day.

O Christmas Tree

Materials

- Christmas Tree repro-ducible (page 32)
- Shapes reproducible (page 33)
- Directions reproducible (page 34)
- scissors
- crayons or markers
- glue

SKILLS: RECOGNIZING AND MATCHING GEOMETRIC SHAPES

Copy a class set of the Christmas Tree reproducible. Copy one Shapes repro-ducible for every two children and one Directions reproducible page. Place the directions on an overhead projector so that children can follow them. Tell chil-dren to color the shapes as indicated on the directions. Then have them cut out and glue their colored shapes to the matching shapes on their "tree." Invite children to color their tree green, and encourage them to describe the colors and shapes of the "ornaments" on it.

Sewing Stockings

Materials

- Stocking reproducible (page 35)
- 8½" x 11" (21.5 cm x 28 cm) red construction paper (two pieces per child)
- scissors
- hole punch
- green yarn, 1 yard (0.9 m) per child
- crayons or markers
- glue
- glitter
- cotton balls

SKILL: DEVELOPING FINE MOTOR SKILLS

Copy on red construction paper two class sets of the Stocking reproducible, and place them at a center along with all the other materials. Tell children to cut out two "stockings" each and to place one stocking cutout on top of the other. Then have them hole-punch the dots around the edges. Ask children to use a piece of yarn to sew their stocking together along three sides (leaving the top open). Invite children to use crayons or markers, glue, glitter, and cotton balls to decorate their stocking with their name and other symbols of Christmas. Display the stockings for a festive holiday environment in the classroom.

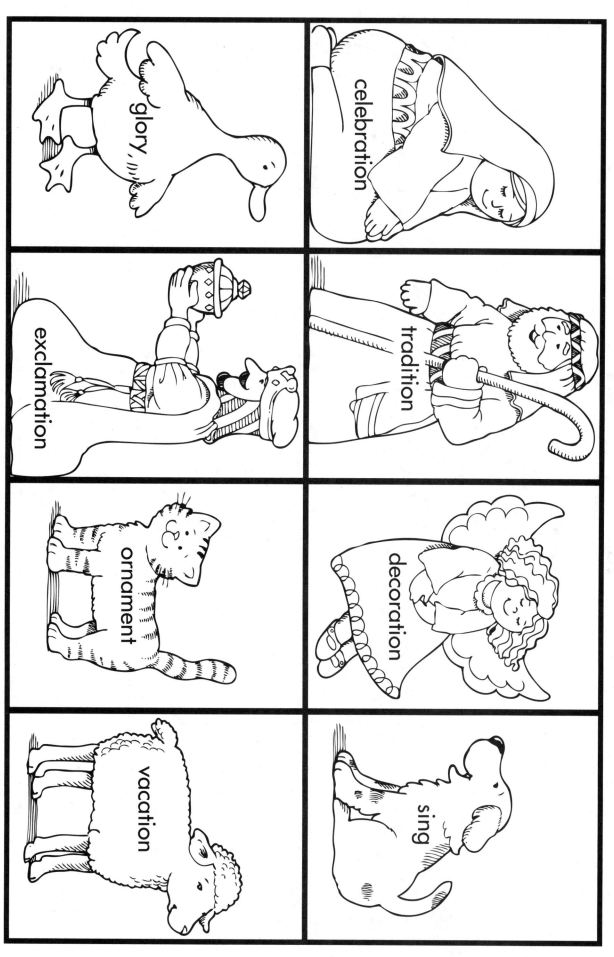

glory

celebration

exclamation

tradition

ornament

decoration

vacation

sing

Stable

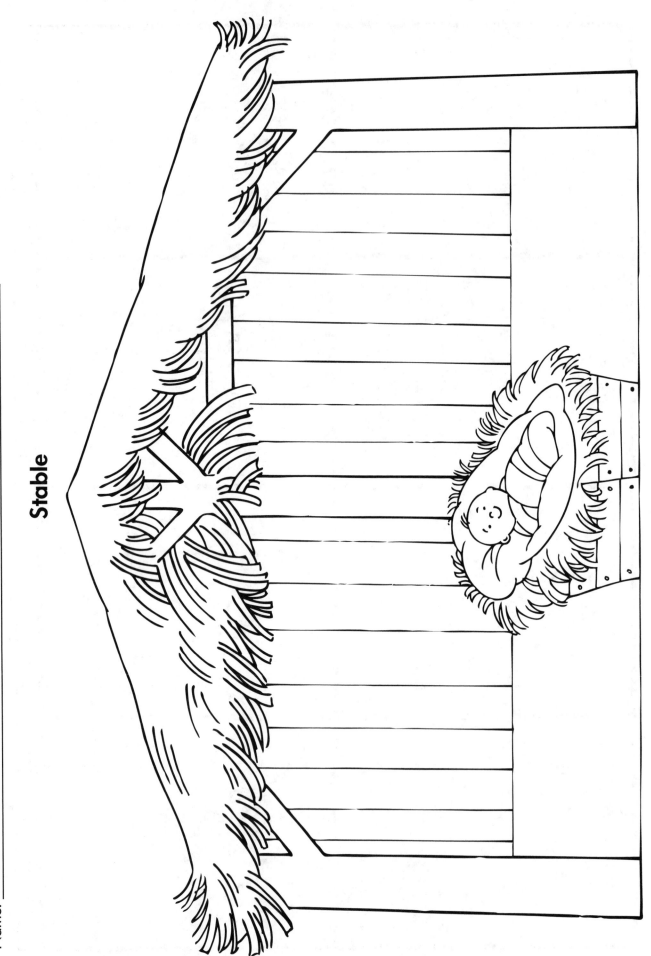

December

Sunday	Monday	Tuesday	Wednesday	Thursday	Friday	Saturday

Name: _____

Christmas Tree

Shapes

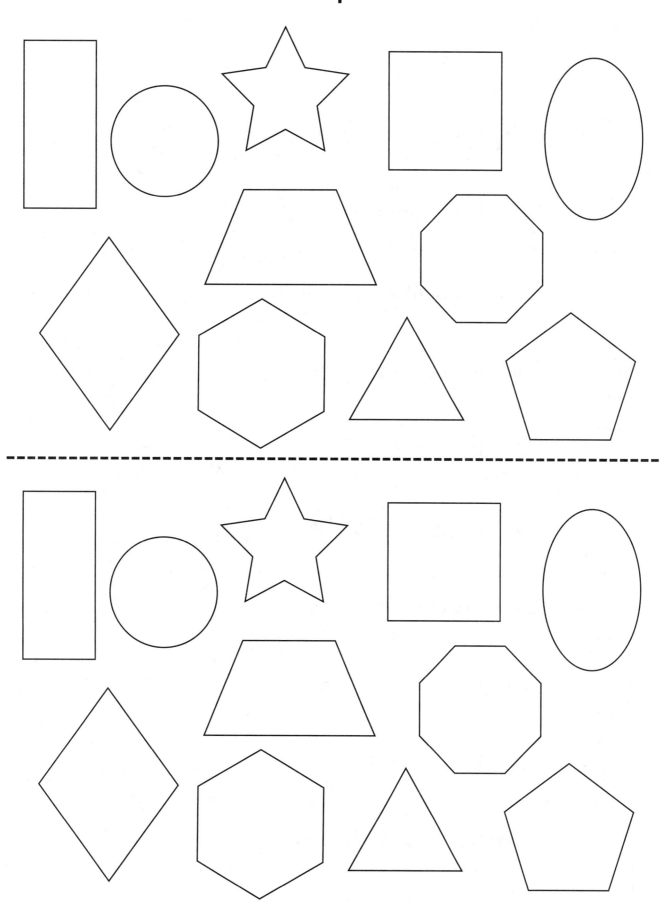

Directions

Color the circle **blue**.

Color the square **red**.

Color the triangle **gray**.

Color the pentagon **orange**.

Color the rectangle **pink**.

Color the oval **purple**.

Color the trapezoid **black**.

Color the diamond **green**.

Color the hexagon **white**.

Color the star **yellow**.

Color the octagon **brown**.

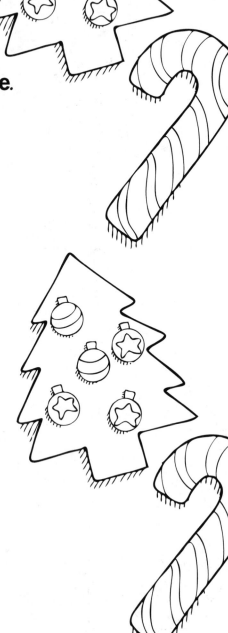

Stocking

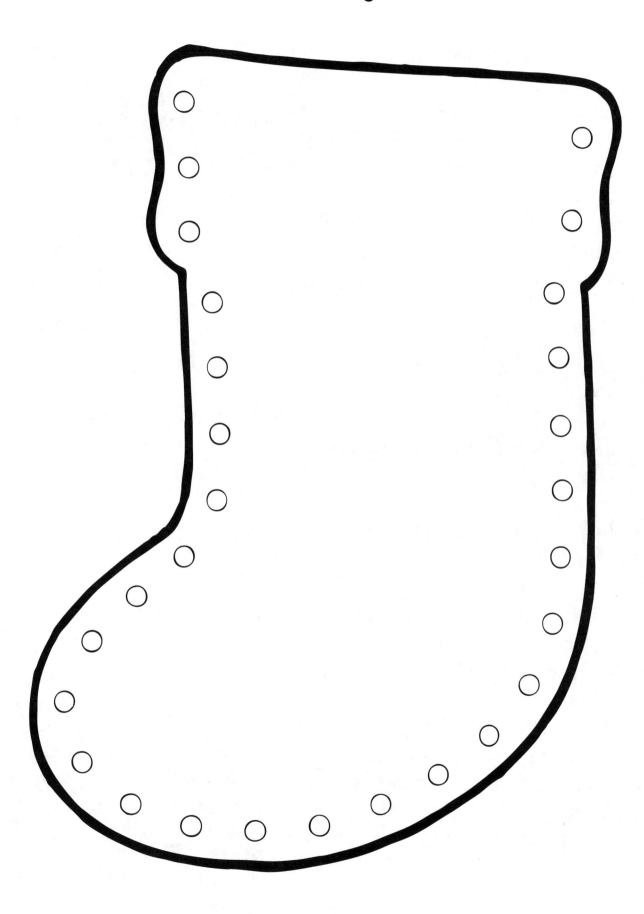

During Martin Luther King Jr.'s lifetime, people were not all treated the same. **Dr. King dreamed of making the world a better place.**

He wanted every person to have the same chance to go to school.
He wanted every person to have the same chance to get a job.
He wanted everyone to be friends.

He wanted everyone to be treated the same.
He wanted the world to be fair to everyone.

Dr. King helped make the world a better place.
He explained how to treat people fairly.

He helped change unfair laws.
He wrote books about equality.

Dr. King helped people work together to make changes.
He helped change the world without fighting.
He helped change the world without war.

Dr. King saw these changes begin to make the world a better place.
And we see them all around us today.
How can you help make the world a better place?

Instant Lessons

Phonemic Awareness

Isolating Phonemes

Invite children to listen to the beginning sound of some words from the reproducible story. Say *work*, *changes*, and *war*. Ask children which word has a different beginning sound. Do the same with *these*, *chance*, and *the*. Repeat the steps to have children identify words with a different middle sound, using sets of words such as *people*, *treated*, *same*; and *making*, *world*, *place*.

Phonics

R-controlled Vowels

Tell children that *word* and *person* have r-controlled vowels. Read aloud the reproducible story, and invite children to raise their hand when they hear a word with an r-controlled vowel (e.g., *Martin*, *Luther*, *during*). Reread the story, and stop each time you say a word with an r-controlled vowel. Invite children to underline the words on their page. Write on the board the words, and underline the "vowel + *r*" spelling pattern in each. Ask children to name other words with r-controlled vowels, and write them on the board.

Fluency

Choral Reading

Read aloud the reproducible story once. Then invite children to follow along as you reread the story. Encourage them to read aloud the words they know. Read the book to children a third time, and ask them to read aloud with you. Read the story with children three to five times over several days to improve fluency.

Vocabulary

Extending Meaning

Write *equality* on the board, ask children what it means, and write their ideas in a web around the word. Then use it in a sentence, such as *Equality means that everyone is treated fairly*. Invite volunteers to complete the sentence frame *Equality is _____*. Mention *equality* in other contexts to give children additional opportunities to learn the word's meaning.

Comprehension

Monitoring Comprehension

Ask children questions such as *What was Martin Luther King Jr.'s Dream?* and *What are some things he did to make his dream come true?* Refer to the boldfaced type to give children clues about where to look for the information that answers these questions. Then lead a brief class discussion about how we can help make the world a better place.

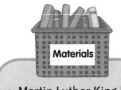
Wheel of Words

SKILLS: IDENTIFYING BASE WORDS AND SUFFIXES

Make a class set of the Martin Luther King Jr. reproducible. Have children cut around the face, and help them cut out the five small boxes in the wheel on the face. Then ask children to cut apart the Suffix Wheel. Have them place the face wheel on top of the Suffix Wheel, and show children how to use a paper fastener to attach the wheels through the center. Read with children the words on the top wheel. Ask children to turn the wheel and read the 15 new words created by the different suffixes. Have them write the words on a piece of paper. Invite children to choose 3 new words from their list and use them in sentences.

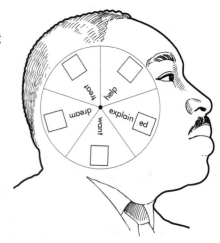

Dr. King's Dream

SKILLS: WRITING AND REVISING PARAGRAPHS

Copy a class set of the Changing Our World reproducible. Discuss with children how Martin Luther King Jr. changed the world. Ask them to name ways they can make the world a better place, and invite children to write their ideas on a piece of paper. Help them revise their first draft into a fluent paragraph. Have children write their final draft on the Changing Our World reproducible. Encourage children to illustrate their work. Bind together children's work in a class book titled "Dr. King's Dream."

Time Line of Dr. King's Life

SKILLS: DEVELOPING NUMBER SENSE AND SEQUENCING EVENTS

Materials

- Time Line reproducible (page 42)
- scissors
- glue
- crayons or markers

Give each child a Time Line reproducible. Explain to children how a time line shows important events from a person's life in the order they happened. Ask children to tell you what they see in each picture at the bottom of the page. Read each caption to children. Help them use the dates to decide the order of events. Have children cut apart the boxes and glue them in the proper spaces on the time line. Invite children to color the time line. To extend learning, ask children to brainstorm what other events might be included on such a time line (e.g., high school/college graduations).

Kingly Words

SKILL: USING NEW VOCABULARY WORDS

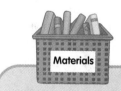

Materials

- MLK Jr. Silhouette reproducible (page 43)
- brown construction paper
- scissors
- glitter-glue

Copy a class set of the MLK Jr. Silhouette reproducible on brown construction paper, and place the copies at a center with other supplies. Have children cut apart the silhouette. Write *change, dream, fair, world, equality,* and *freedom* on the board. Discuss with children how each of these words relates to Martin Luther King Jr. Invite children to add their own words to the list. Ask children to choose at least three words from the list and use glitter-glue to write them on their silhouette.

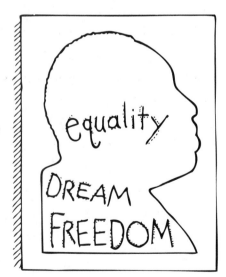

Martin Luther King Jr.

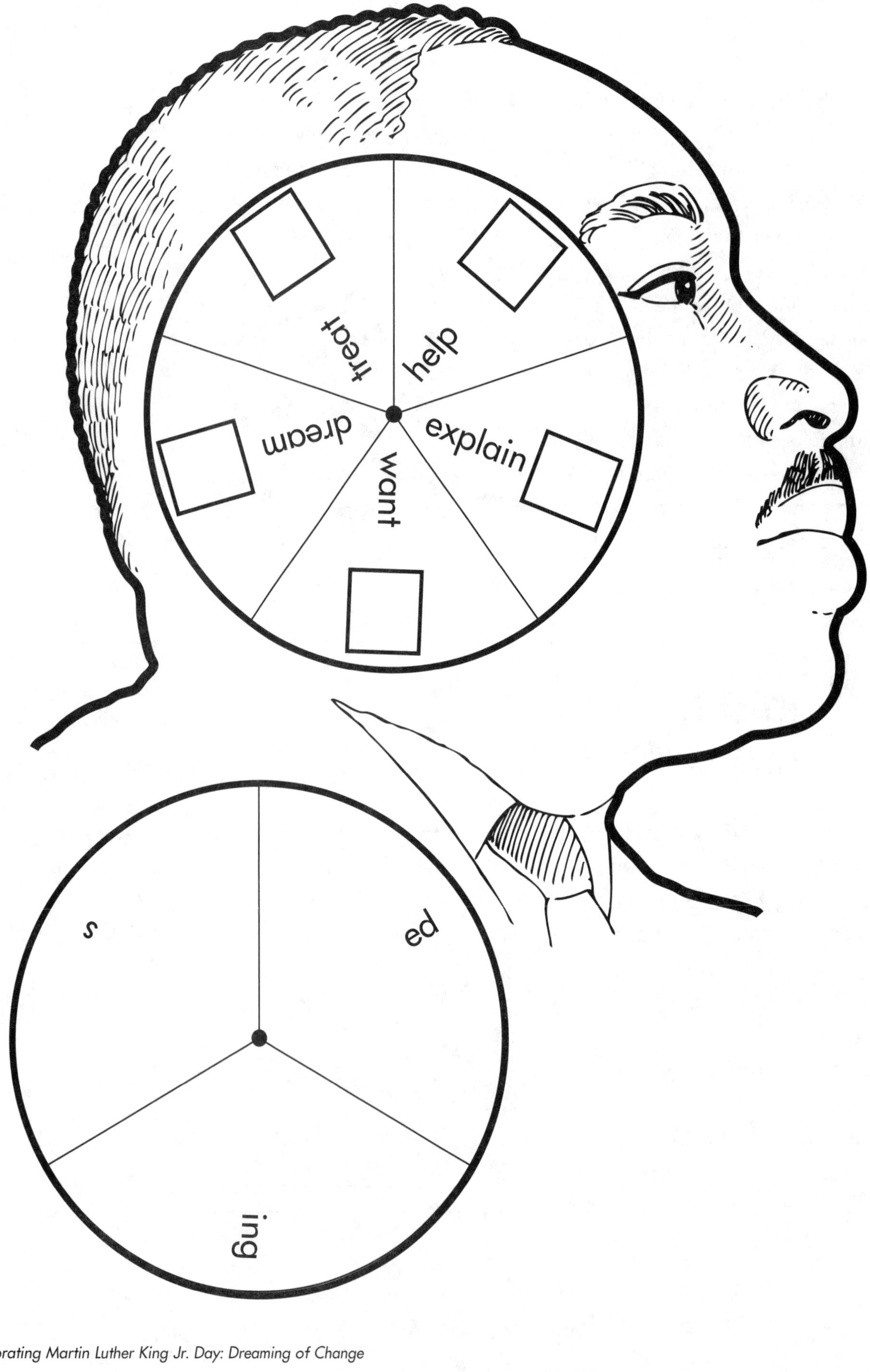

treat

help

dream

explain

want

Suffix Wheel

s

ed

ing

Name: _____

Changing Our World

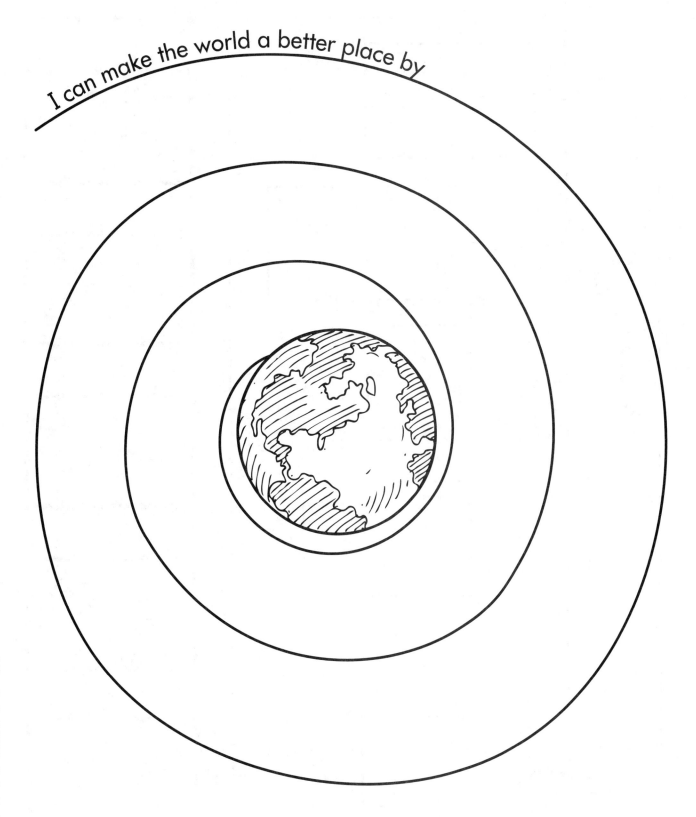

I can make the world a better place by

Time Line

1929

1968

1953—
Marries
Coretta Scott

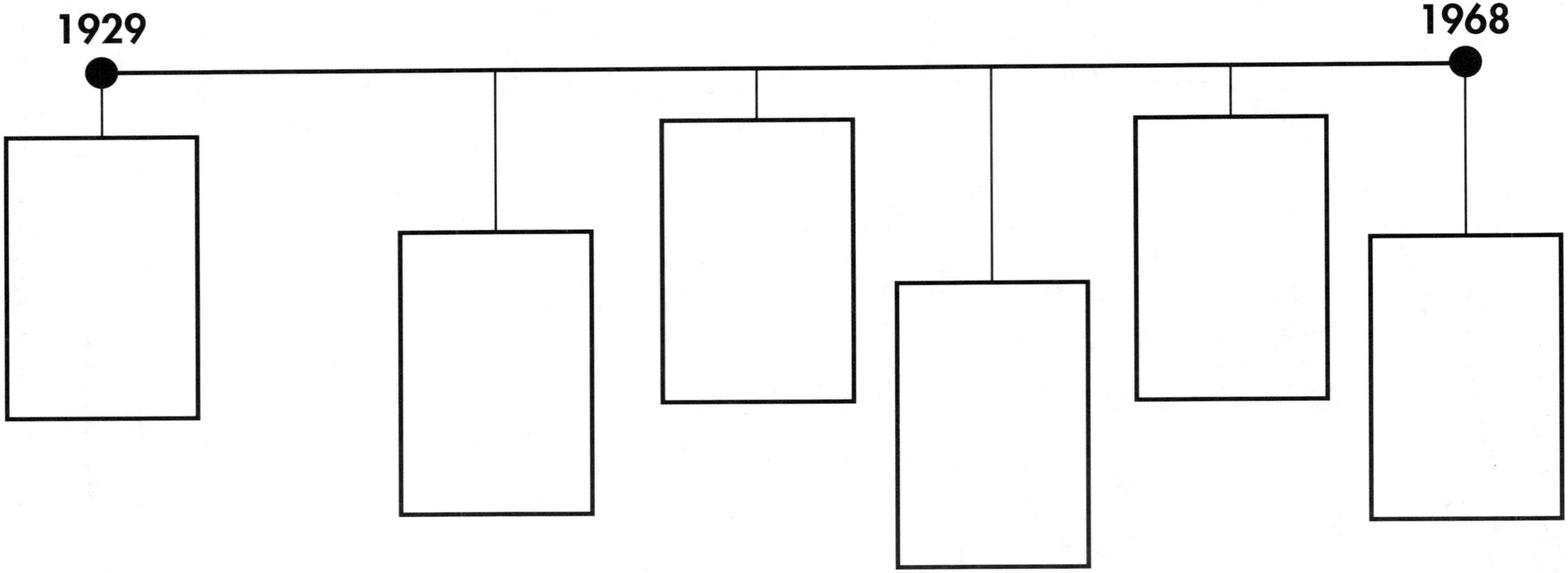

1964—Wins
Nobel Peace
Prize

1958—First
book published

Stride Toward Freedom

1963—"I have
a dream"
speech

1968—
Assassinated

Rev. Martin Luther King Jr.

1929—Born

MLK Jr. Silhouette

My friend Nick celebrates Chinese New Year.
He is Chinese American.
Chinese New Year comes in January and February.
It lasts for 15 days.

Before New Year's Day, Nick helps his family
  clean the house.
This gets rid of all the back luck from last year.
They put up red **decorations**.
Red is a lucky color.

Nick's family cooks a lot of food for New
  Year's Eve dinner.
Nick's family gives him and his sister red
  envelopes.
The envelopes have money inside.
Everyone gets a haircut and wears new clothes.

Nick invited me to a **parade** on the last day
  of the old year.
There were dancers, firecrackers, and music.
Dragon dancers danced down the street.
One person held the dragon's head.
Many people held the long body.

The **dragon** is a sign of good luck.
The dance celebrates the beginning of spring.

The firecrackers come after the dragon dance.
Lanterns light up the night sky.
Everyone says *Gung hay fat choy* to wish
  each other a happy new year!

Instant Lessons

Phonemic Awareness

Phoneme Blending

Say /a/ /n/ /d/, and invite children to blend the phonemes to make the word *and*. Repeat the sounds, and write the corresponding letters on the board. Ask children to help you read the word. Repeat the steps with other words from the reproducible story, including *lasts*, *gets*, *red*, *rid*, and *helps*.

Phonics

Short *i* and Long *i* Vowel Sounds

Draw a vertical line down the middle of a piece of chart paper. Write *Short i* at the top of the left-hand column and *Long i* at the top of the right-hand column. Tell children to listen for the short *i* sound as you say *Nick* and *is*. Write the words in the left-hand column. Invite children to name other words with the short *i* sound, and add them to the column on the left. Tell children to listen for the long *i* sound, and say *Chinese* and *light*. Write the words in the right-hand column. Invite children to name other words with the long *i* sound, and add them to the column on the right. Ask children to help you reread both lists.

Fluency

Tape-Assisted Reading

Read the reproducible story into a tape recorder. Place the tape, the tape recorder, and the reproducible at a center. Invite children to follow the text as they listen to the story. Have children listen to the tape again and read aloud with the story. Encourage children to practice reading the story as they listen to the tape until they can read the text fluently.

Vocabulary

Repeated Exposure to Words

Read the boldfaced words on the reproducible story (i.e., *decorations*, *envelopes*, *parade*, *dragon*, and *lanterns*) with the children. Ask children to tell what they know about each word, and encourage them to use the pictures as clues to word meanings when possible. Ask volunteers to use the words in sentences.

Comprehension

Answering Questions

Divide the class into small groups, and ask them to use their reproducible story to answer the following questions: *Why do Nick and his family clean the house before Chinese New Year? What is special about the red envelopes Nick and his sister receive? What does the dragon dance celebrate? Is luck important to Nick's family?* Invite each group to answer aloud one of the questions. Have children point to the text that answers the question.

Good Luck Banners

SKILL: IDENTIFYING PRESENT- AND PAST-TENSE VERBS

Materials

- Celebrating Chinese New Year: Nick's New Year reproducible (page 44)
- Flags reproducible (page 48)
- red construction paper
- scissors
- tape
- yarn (one long piece, allow 10" [25.5 cm] per student)

Copy a class set of the Flags reproducible on red construction paper. Write *lasts*, *celebrates*, *clean*, *cooks*, and *wish* in a column on the board. Ask children to find the sentences on their reproducible story that contain these words. Read aloud the sentences, emphasizing the words listed on the board. Ask for volunteers to change the sentences so that the words listed on the board are used in the past-tense form. Show children how to change the end of each word to make it past tense (i.e., drop the *s* and add *-d* or *-ed*), and write the new words in a second column on the board. Invite children to use three of the present-tense verbs in new sentences. Ask them to write their sentences on the Present-Tense Flag. Then have children change those sentences to past tense and write them on their Past-Tense Flag. Invite children to cut apart their flags, and help them tape the flags onto one long piece of yarn to create a classroom banner. Hang the banner over children's desks or above the chalkboard.

Present Tense
Say "Gung Hay Fat Choy"
to wish someone a
happy new year!

New Year Cheer

SKILL: WRITING STEPS IN A PROCESS

Materials

- Celebrating Chinese New Year: Nick's New Year reproducible (page 44)
- How to Celebrate Chinese New Year reproducible (page 49)

Make a class set of the How to Celebrate Chinese New Year reproducible. Place the pages at a center. Ask children to review the steps for celebrating Chinese New Year as outlined in the reproducible story. Invite children to write or dictate these steps on the How to Celebrate Chinese New Year reproducible.

Follow the steps below to have a great Chinese New Year!

1. Clean the house.
2. Put up red decorations.
3. _____
4. _____
5. _____
6. _____

Gung Hay Fat Choy

恭賀新禧

Money Math

SKILLS: ADDING AND SUBTRACTING MONEY

Materials

- Money reproducible (page 50)
- green copy paper
- scissors
- marker
- 12 small red envelopes

Copy the Money reproducible on green paper, and cut apart the "bills." Use a marker to write on separate envelopes a simple addition or subtraction problem that matches the amount on each bill. Place each bill in its corresponding envelope. Arrange the envelopes in a pile at a center. Invite groups of three to four children to the center. Ask children to take an envelope one at a time from the top of the pile. Have children read the math problem and say aloud the answer. Ask them to look at the number on the bill inside the envelope to check their work. When children answer correctly, ask them to replace the envelope. If children answer incorrectly, have them say aloud twice the problem and answer before replacing the envelope.

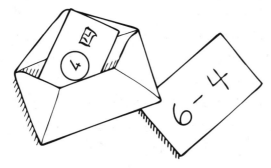

Dazzling Dragons

SKILL: DEVELOPING FINE MOTOR SKILLS

Materials

- Dragon reproducible (page 51)
- crayons or markers
- scissors
- tape
- tissue paper scraps
- glue
- craft sticks

Copy a class set of the Dragon reproducible. Give a reproducible to each child to color and cut out. Show children how to tape together the two sections to make one long body. Have children cut eight to ten tissue paper triangles and glue them along the bottom of the dragon's body. Ask children to crumple small scraps of tissue paper into balls and arrange them in a pattern in separate sections of the dragon's body. Have children glue the balls in place. Give each child two craft sticks. Tell children to glue the sticks to the back of the dragon to create handles. When the glue is dry, encourage children to make their dragons "dance."

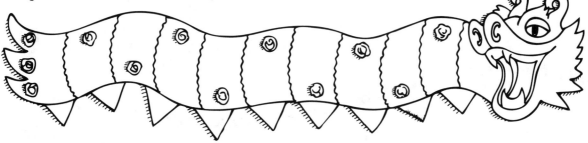

Flags

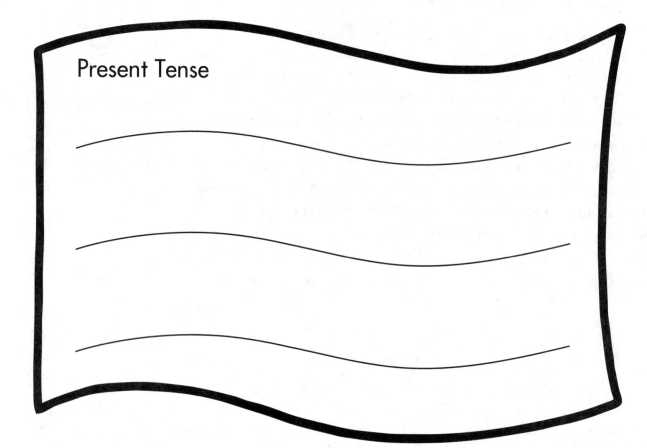

Present Tense

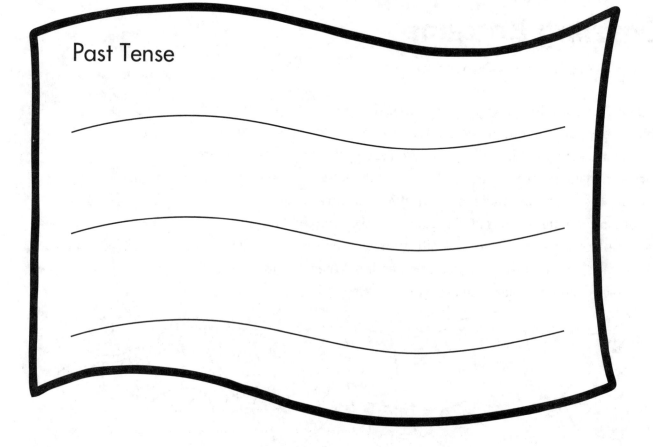

Past Tense

Name: _____

How to Celebrate Chinese New Year

Follow the steps below to have a great Chinese New Year!

1. _____

2. _____

3. _____

4. _____

5. _____

6. _____

Gung Hay Fat Choy

恭贺新禧

Money

一 (1) 一	一 (1) 一
二 (2) 二	二 (2) 二
三 (3) 三	三 (3) 三
四 (4) 四	四 (4) 四
五 (5) 五	五 (5) 五
六 (6) 六	六 (6) 六

Dragon

Valentine's Day is on February 14. It is a day to show special people that you care about them.

I give my mom a big box of candy. She is my valentine because she tucks me in at night.

I give my dad a card I made for him. He is my valentine because he helped me learn to tie my shoes.

I give my teacher a flower. She is my valentine because she teaches me to read.

I give cards to all of my friends at school. They are my valentines because we have fun playing together.

I give gifts to my valentines so they know I care about them. That makes them feel happy.

It is fun to make people happy! My valentines smile and give me hugs. **Sometimes, they even give me gifts, too!**

Instant Lessons

Phonemic Awareness

Phoneme Segmentation

Ask children to tap or clap to count the number of sounds they hear in *it*, *that*, *mom*, *candy*, and *teaches*. Repeat the sounds as you write on the board the letters for each word. Explain that sometimes two letters come together to make one sound (e.g., *th* in *that*). When the list is complete, invite children to help you read aloud the words.

Phonics

Recognizing Singular and Plural Nouns

Explain to children that a singular noun refers to one person, place, or thing. Write *Singular* on chart paper. Ask children to find singular nouns on their reproducible story, such as *valentine*, *day*, *night*, *card*, and *teacher*. Write the words under "Singular" on the chart. Write *Plural* at the top of another column on the chart paper. Add *s* to *valentine*, and explain that when *s* is added to the end of a word, the word becomes plural. Add *s* to each word on the list of nouns, and write them in the "Plural" column. Then ask children to find and underline other plural nouns on the reproducible story (e.g., *shoes*, *cards*, *friends*, *gifts*, *hugs*).

Fluency

Reader's Theater

Divide the class into groups of three. Explain to children that they will take turns reading two sentences at a time from the reproducible story. Tell them that when each child has read twice, they should then read only one sentence. Ask children to practice reading from the "script." Remind them to read expressively and listen to other readers. Encourage children to perform the actions as they read the story. After the groups have rehearsed, ask them to perform for the class.

Vocabulary

Synonyms

Locate *special* on the reproducible story. Invite children to think of as many words as they can that have the same meaning. Have them place each synonym in the sentence frame *It is a day to show _____ people that you care about them.*

Comprehension

Generating Questions

Have children think of a question that can be answered by reading the text of the reproducible story. Divide the class into teams. Invite Team A to ask Team B one of their questions. Award Team B one point if they answer the question correctly. Alternate teams until no questions remain. Give to the winning team heart stickers or other small prizes.

- Celebrating Valentine's Day: My Special Valentines reproducible (page 52)
- Follow the Path to Your Valentine's Heart reproducible (pages 56–57)
- tape
- die
- game markers (coins or counters)

The Path to My Heart

SKILL: RECOGNIZING WORDS WITH CONSONANT DIGRAPHS *CH*, *SH*, *TH*, AND *WH*

Copy the Follow the Path to Your Valentine's Heart reproducible pages, and tape them together. Place the game board at a center with a die and game markers. Invite groups of two to three children to the center. Ask children to take turns rolling a die and moving their game piece that number of spaces. Tell children to read the word below their game piece and to try to find it on their reproducible story. Tell children to take another turn if they can find their word. Have them pass to the next player if they cannot find their word (not all words will appear on the reproducible story). Explain to children that the first player to reach the end of the path wins the game.

- Happy Valentine's Day reproducible (page 58)
- valentine heart candies
- glue
- red, pink, or white construction paper
- glitter
- ribbon
- stickers

Sweet Sayings

SKILL: WRITING SENTENCES

Copy a class set of the Happy Valentine's Day reproducible. Invite children to think of someone special they would like to give a greeting card to. Have them write that person's name on the first blank line of the paper. Then ask them to complete the sentence. Show children some of the sayings on the heart candies. Invite them to think of similar phrases they might say to their card recipient. Encourage children to fill in the blank hearts on the reproducible with their sayings and then write a note to their valentine on the lines provided. Tell children to cut around the card, and have them glue their paper to a piece of construction paper. Show them how to fold the card so that the message is on the inside. Have children use glitter, ribbon, stickers, and valentine heart candies to decorate their construction paper cover.

"Half" a Heart

SKILL: MATCHING FRACTIONS

Copy, color, and cut out the Heart Fractions and Heart Cards reproducible pages. For a self-checking feature, write on the back of each Heart Card the fraction that is represented. Place the Heart Fractions and Heart Cards at a center. Invite groups of two to the center. Ask children to match the Heart Fractions with the Heart Cards that represent the same amounts. Have children check their work when they are finished.

Materials
- Heart Fractions reproducible (pages 59)
- Heart Cards reproducible (page 60)
- crayons or markers
- scissors

 =  or

Happy Heartstrings

SKILL: FOLLOWING DIRECTIONS

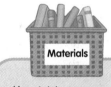

Copy a class set of the Heartstrings reproducible, and ask children to color a different pattern or design in each space. Tell children to cut off the top and bottom of the page along the dotted lines. Then have them fold their paper along Line A. Show children how to accordion-fold Lines B and C (so that the edges of the paper meet the fold of Line A). Have children cut along the dotted lines of the Heartstrings reproducible to make two strips of heart cutouts. Invite children to fill in the "To" line and write their name on the "From" line. Have them tape together their strips to make one long heartstring.

Materials
- Heartstrings reproducible (page 61)
- crayons or markers
- scissors
- tape

Follow the Path to Your Valentine's Heart

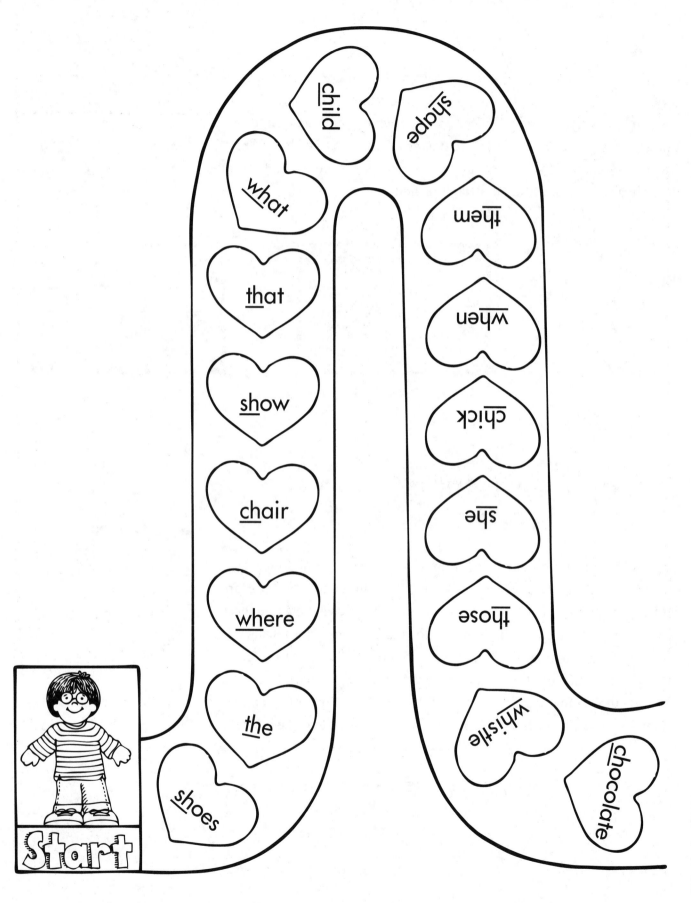

child

shape

what

them

that

when

show

chick

chair

she

where

those

the

whistle

shoes

chocolate

Start

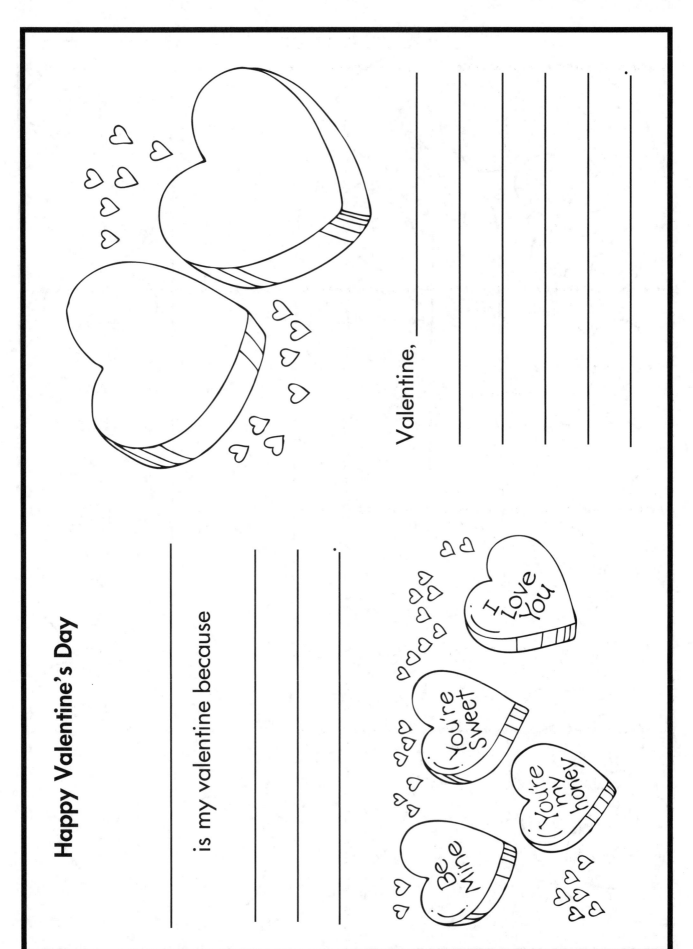

Happy Valentine's Day

is my valentine because _____

Valentine, _____

Heart Fractions

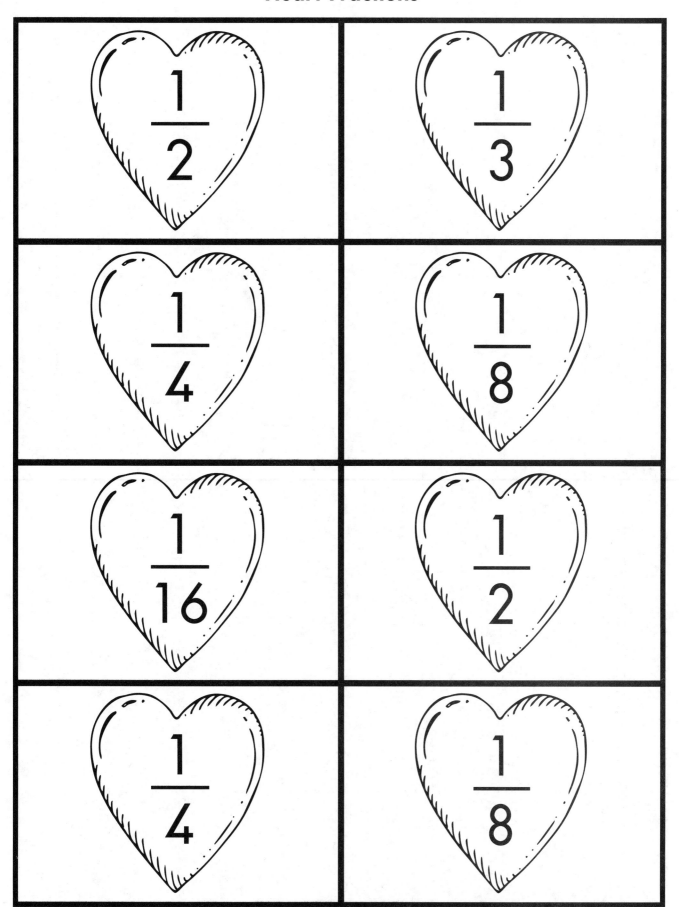

Heart Cards

Heartstrings

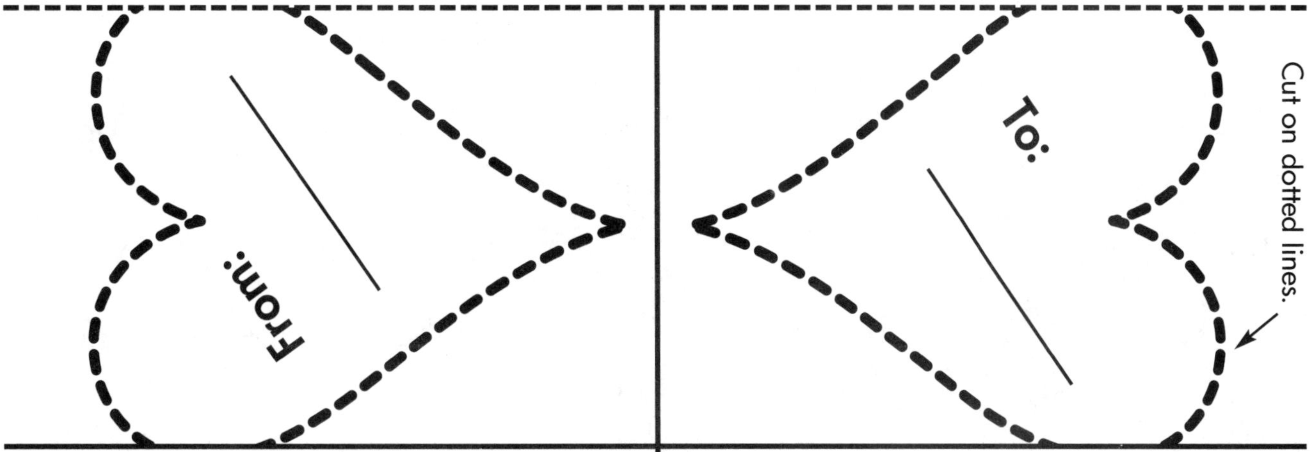

From:

To:

Cut on dotted lines.

Line B

Line A

Line C

What is a president?
The President is a leader who plans what is best
    for our country.
You can be a leader, too.

The President is a helper who helps people in need.
You can be a helper, too.

What is a president?
The President is a problem solver who works
    with other countries.
You can be a problem solver, too.

The President is a community builder who helps
    people live and work together.
You can be a community builder, too.

What is a president?
The President is a teacher who teaches us about
    what is happening around the world.
You can be a teacher, too.

The President is a decision maker who helps our
    country make good choices.
You can help make important decisions, too.

What is a president?
The President is a lawmaker who makes
    laws to keep our country safe.
You can help make laws, too.

The President is the leader of our country.
Someday, you could be the President, too.

Instant Lessons

 **Phonemic Awareness**

Phoneme Blending

Say /c/ /a/ /n/, and invite children to blend the phonemes to make *can*. Repeat the sounds, and write the corresponding letters on the board. Ask children to help you read the word. Repeat the steps with other words from the reproducible story, such as *plans*, *best*, and *helps*.

 **Phonics**

Short *e* and Long *e* Vowel Sounds

Write *best* and *leader* on the board, and emphasize the difference between the short *e* and long *e* sounds. Ask children to find all the words containing a short or long *e* sound on their reproducible story. Write the words on the board. Give children a piece of paper, and help them fold it four times to create a grid with 16 boxes. Tell children to write *Short e* in the first box, *Long e* in the second box, and the words from the board in the remaining 14 boxes. Tell them to cut apart the boxes to make cards. Ask children to use the short *e* and long *e* cards as column headings, and have children arrange the remaining cards in the appropriate columns.

 **Fluency**

Student-Adult Reading

Invite several adults from your school (e.g., the secretary, the principal, the custodian, parent volunteers) to help your class with fluency. Pair a child with an adult, and ask the adult to read the reproducible story to the child to model fluency. Then invite the child to read aloud. Encourage the adult to help the child when necessary. Have the child read the story several times until he or she reads it fluently.

 **Vocabulary**

Extending Meaning

Write on the board the following words from the reproducible story: *leader*, *problem solver*, *community builder*, *decision maker*, and *lawmaker*. Read and reread the words with the children. Ask children to tell what the words mean and to think of people who demonstrate each quality. Invite children to think of ways they could show attributes of each quality at home and at school. Have children write their ideas for each word.

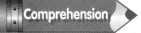 **Comprehension**

Summarizing

Tell children that a summary includes only the most important information. Encourage children to reread the story several times to look for qualities a president might have. Write their ideas on chart paper. Then have children use the ideas to write their own paragraph summarizing the qualities of a good president.

Word Builder

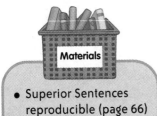

Materials

- Superior Sentences reproducible (page 66)
- scissors
- glue

SKILL: USING WORD PARTS

Copy a class set of the Superior Sentences reproducible. Have children use a pencil to complete with *-er* or *-r* each word card at the bottom of the page to make a new word. Ask children to cut apart the cards. Encourage children to read aloud the sentences and use their new words to complete the sentences. Have children glue the words in place after you have checked them with the class.

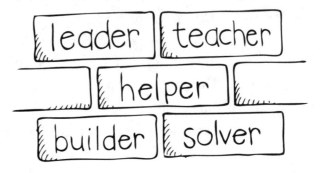

Persuasive Presidents

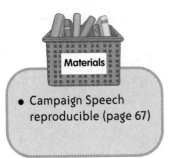

Materials

- Campaign Speech reproducible (page 67)

SKILL: WRITING A PERSUASIVE PARAGRAPH

Copy a class set of the Campaign Speech reproducible. Discuss with children how presidential candidates give speeches to try to persuade others to vote for them. Invite children to brainstorm the qualities they possess that would make them a good president. Encourage children to think of things they do that demonstrate qualities of good leadership. Have them use these ideas to write a campaign speech on the reproducible. When they are finished, invite children to read aloud their speeches, and then hold a mock election to vote for a class president for the day.

Prompt Presidents

SKILL: TELLING TIME (ANALOG AND DIGITAL)

Copy the Pocket Watches and Wristwatches reproducible pages. Draw hands for each watch on the Pocket Watches reproducible. Then write the digital form of the same times on the Wristwatches reproducible. For a self-checking feature, write the digital time on the back of each "pocket watch." Cut apart the pages, and place the pieces at a center. Explain to children that past presidents used pocket watches to tell time, while modern presidents use wristwatches. Have children match the analog and digital times on the watches. Ask them to turn over the pocket watches to check their work.

Materials

- Pocket Watches reproducible (page 68)
- Wristwatches reproducible (page 69)
- scissors

Crafty Cabins

SKILLS: FOLLOWING DIRECTIONS AND WRITING A PARAGRAPH

Copy a class set of the Log Cabin reproducible on card stock. Have children cut out the log cabin and the young Abe Lincoln figure. Tell children to cut along the dotted lines on the door and glue the Abe Lincoln cutout to the back so it is visible when the door is open. Invite children to glue pretzel sticks for "logs" to their "cabin." Discuss with children what Abraham Lincoln's childhood in a log cabin must have been like. Ask them to write a paragraph about it on handwriting paper. Invite children to cut out and glue the log cabin and their paragraph to a piece of construction paper.

Materials

- Log Cabin reproducible (page 70)
- card stock
- scissors
- glue
- pretzel sticks
- handwriting paper
- 12" x 18" (30.5 cm x 46 cm) construction paper

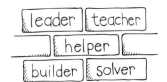

Superior Sentences

The child at the front of the line is the [   ] .

A person who makes a home is a [   ] .

A person who makes the rules people
need to live by is a [   ] .

If you can't do something by yourself,
ask for a [   ] .

A person who can find a solution to a
problem is a problem [   ] .

A person who helps others learn is a [   ] .

lead_____	help_____	solve_____
build_____	lawmake_____	teach_____

Name: _____

Campaign Speech

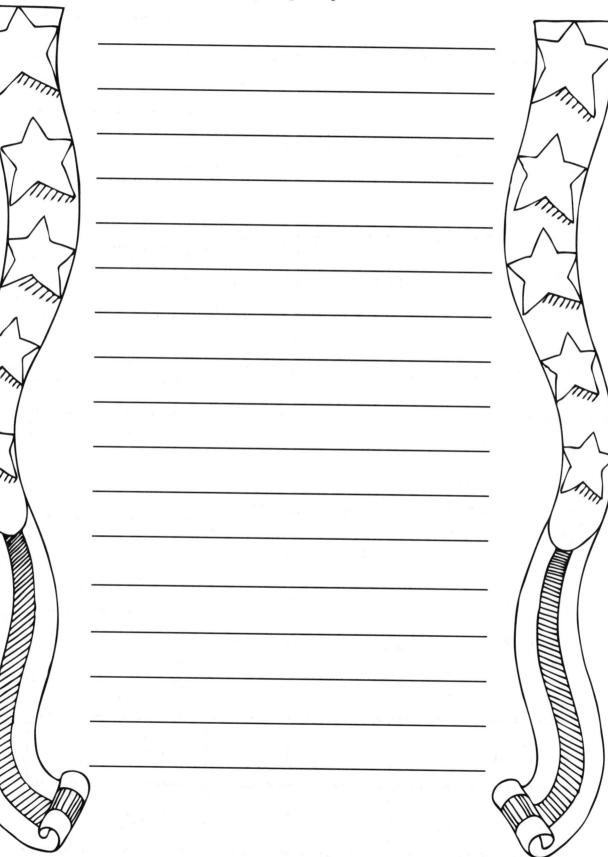

Pocket Watches

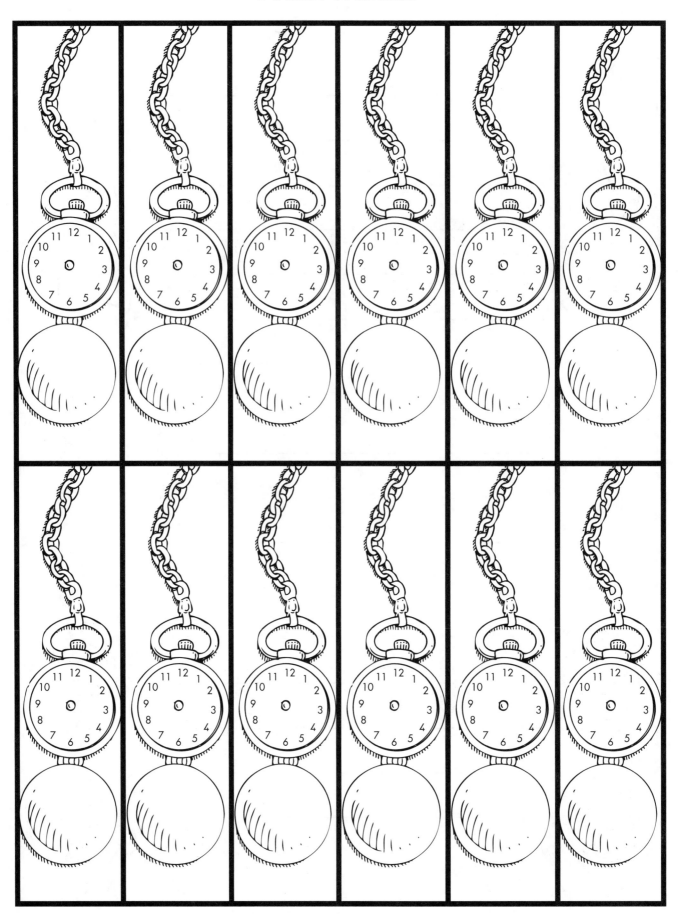

Wristwatches

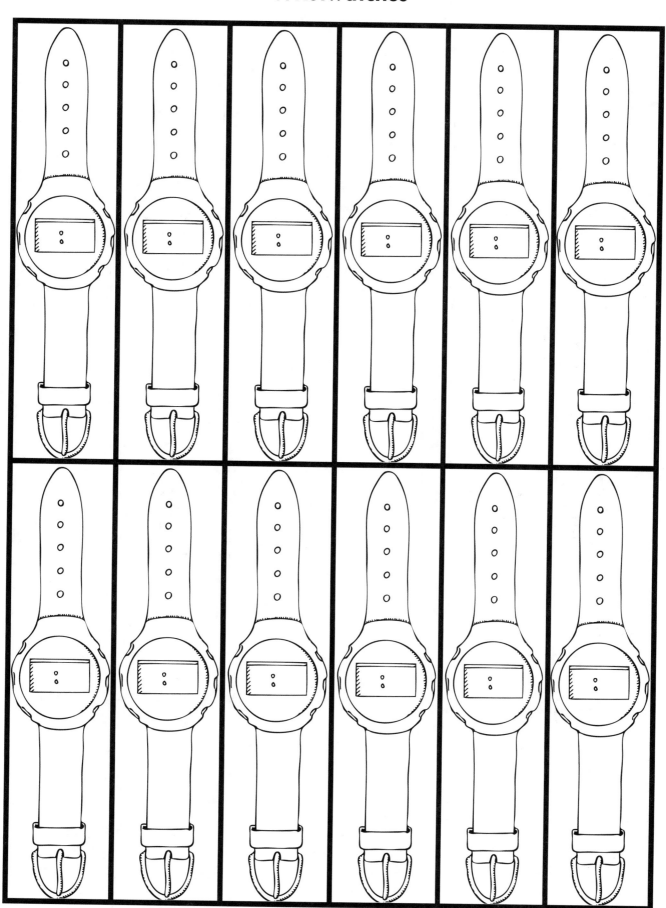

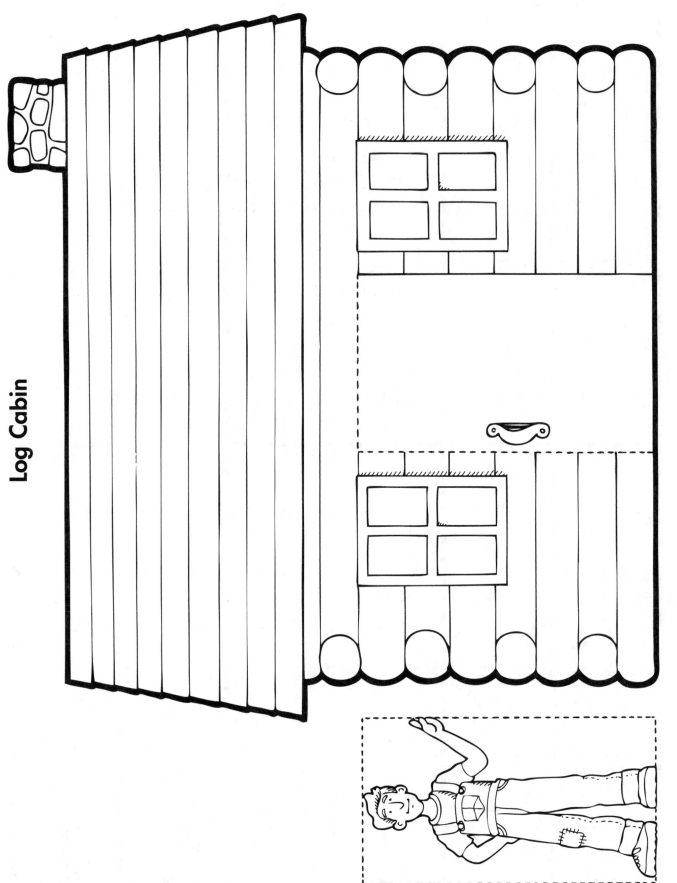

Log Cabin

Easter comes at the beginning of spring.
It is a special time for many people.

Some people paint eggs.
Some people plant Easter lilies.
Some people think of the Easter Bunny.
These are all **symbols** of Easter.

What do these symbols mean?
Many Easter symbols make people think of springtime and new life.

Eggs are symbols of new life because some
brand-new baby animals come out of them.
Bunnies are symbols of the springtime moon.
Easter falls on the first Sunday after the first
full moon after the first day of spring.

Easter lilies are symbols of new life and
springtime.
Easter lilies start to bloom around Easter time.
New clothes are a symbol of new life, too.
Some people get a new outfit for Easter.

The cross is a symbol of Jesus Christ
and new life.
For Christians, Easter is the celebration
of His Resurrection.
All of these symbols remind us that
it's a special time for many people.
It's time for Easter!

Instant Lessons

Phonemic Awareness

Phoneme Segmentation

Ask children to tap or clap to count the number of sounds they hear in *think*, *plant*, *them*, *brand*, *after*, and *bloom*. Repeat the sounds as you write the letters for each word on the board. When the list is complete, invite children to help you read aloud the words.

Phonics

The Long *e* Vowel Combination -*ea*

Write *Easter* on the board, and ask children to identify the beginning vowel sound. Show children that the long *e* sound is spelled -*ea*. Invite children to find and circle *Easter* on their reproducible story. Ask children to name other words with long *e* spelled -*ea* (e.g., *clean, eat, feast)*, and write them on the board. Have each child use two words from the list to write and illustrate a sentence about Easter.

Fluency

Partner Reading

Pair fluent readers (perhaps from an upper grade level) with children, and ask them to read the stories together. Ask the experienced reader to read the first section to model fluent reading. Then tell the beginning reader to read aloud the same passage. Encourage the fluent reader to help if necessary. Ask the pair to continue reading in this pattern until the beginning reader can read the story fluently.

Vocabulary

Using Context Clues

Ask children to use a yellow marker to highlight *symbol* and the plural form, *symbols,* on their reproducible story. Encourage children to use context clues to write a definition for the word. Ask children to copy from the story one sentence that features *symbol* or *symbols*, and have them explain the sentence. Encourage children to write their own sentence using the word.

Comprehension

Monitoring Comprehension

Have children write on a piece of paper the sentences they do not understand from the story. Tell children to look before and after the sentences for text that will help them determine the meanings. If children still cannot decipher the meanings, encourage them to use a dictionary to help with unfamiliar terms. Then have children rewrite the sentences in their own words.

Bountiful Baskets

SKILL: RECOGNIZING PLURAL WORDS

Materials

- Easter Baskets reproducible (page 75)
- Easter Word Cards reproducible (page 76)
- crayons or markers
- scissors

Copy, color, and cut apart the Easter Baskets and Easter Word Cards reproducible pages. For a self-checking feature, write all of the plural words from the Easter Word Cards on the back of the Easter Basket labeled "Plural"; write the singular words on the back of the Easter Basket labeled "Singular." Place the Easter Baskets and Easter Word Cards at a center. Have children read the words on the Easter Baskets. Explain that a singular noun is one person, place, or thing (e.g., a flower). Explain that a plural noun is more than one thing (e.g., flowers) and usually ends with *s*. Ask children to place the Easter Word Cards with singular words in the "Singular" Easter Basket and the Easter Word Cards with plural words in the "Plural" Easter Basket. Have children turn over the Easter Baskets to check their work.

Job for a Jumper

SKILL: WRITING DESCRIPTIONS

Materials

- Job Description reproducible (page 77)
- crayons or markers

Copy a class set of the Job Description reproducible. Brainstorm with children what a bunny would need to be able to do in order to be the Easter Bunny. Include abilities he should be able to demonstrate, character qualities he should possess, and necessary physical characteristics. Have children use the ideas to write a paragraph. Invite children to draw a picture of the Easter Bunny on their paper.

Pretty Patterns

SKILL: CREATING PATTERNS

Copy one Egg Cards reproducible for every two children and a class set of the Color Patterns reproducible. Give each child a block of twelve egg cards. Invite them to color the "eggs" using six different solid colors (i.e., there should be two eggs of each color), and have students cut apart the cards. Ask children to arrange the cards in a pattern. Give each child a Color Patterns reproducible, and have the children use crayons or markers to copy in Row 1 the pattern they arranged. Then invite children to rearrange their egg cards to create a new pattern and copy it in Row 2. Encourage children to repeat the steps to make five different patterns.

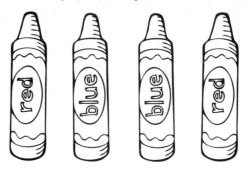

Exquisite Images

SKILL: DEVELOPING FINE MOTOR SKILLS

Copy a class set of the Painted Egg reproducible on card stock. Place the pages at a center. Ask children to look at the decorated Easter "eggs" on the reproducible. Encourage children to use them for ideas to design their own egg. First, have children use pencils to draw the design. Then have them use crayons to color the patterns on their egg. Ask children to press firmly with their crayons. Have them paint over their designs with watercolor paints. When the paint is dry, have children cut out their eggs and display them in the classroom.

Easter Baskets

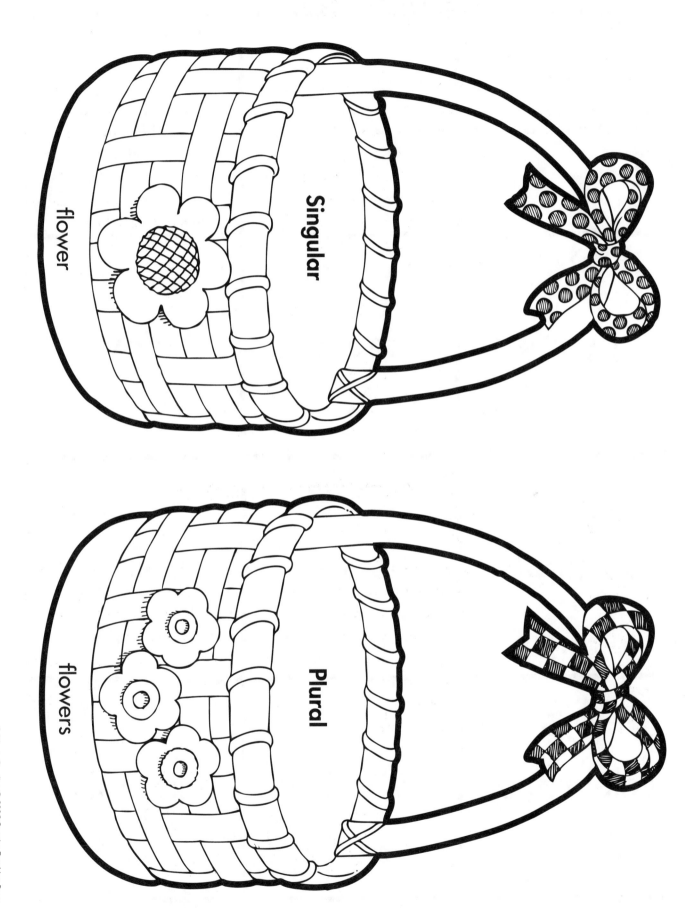

Singular

flower

Plural

flowers

Easter Word Cards

cross	outfit	lilies
people	moon	day
symbols	eggs	bunny
celebration	bunnies	animals

Name: _____

Job Description

Abilities

_____

_____

_____

_____

Character Qualities

_____

_____

_____

_____

Physical Characteristics

_____

_____

_____

_____

_____

_____

_____

_____

Egg Cards

Row 1

Row 2

Row 3

Row 4

Row 5

Painted Egg

Celebrating Cinco de Mayo: Fiesta Time!

Today is the 5th of May.
Let's celebrate Cinco de Mayo!
Let's celebrate victory for Mexico in 1862.
Let's have a fiesta!

The streets are filled with the sights of Cinco de Mayo!
We see colorful dresses and Mexican sombreros.
We see dancers spinning and clapping their hands.

**The streets are filled with the sounds of
    Cinco de Mayo!**
We hear the mariachi band playing and
    singing.
We hear the children cheer when the
    piñata is broken.

**The streets are filled with the smells of
    Cinco de Mayo!**
We smell warm corn tortillas.
We smell spicy beans and rice.

**The streets are filled with the tastes
    of Cinco de Mayo!**
We taste tacos and enchiladas.
We taste sweet treats that fall from
    the piñata.

There is a feeling of pride in the streets on Cinco de Mayo,
    and we show it!

Instant Lessons

Phonemic Awareness

Phoneme Deletion and Addition

Invite children to follow along as you read aloud the story. Tell children to point to the word *playing* on their reproducible story. Ask children to delete the /p/ sound and say the new word (i.e., *laying*). Name other words from the text, and tell children to delete or add a sound to make a new word.

Phonics

The Suffix *-ing*

Ask children to find on their reproducible story the words that end with *-ing* (e.g., *spinning*, *clapping*). Write the words on the board, and invite volunteers to remove *-ing* to reveal the base word. Explain that sometimes the final consonant is doubled before adding *-ing*. Ask children to pick a word (e.g., *spinning*) and to write a sentence for it. Tell children to remove *-ing* from the word and to write a sentence using the base word. Then have them repeat the steps with another word.

Fluency

Tape-Assisted Reading

Audiotape yourself or another special person from your school (e.g., the principal) reading the story. Play the tape, and tell children to run their fingers under the text on their reproducible page as they listen. Play the tape again several times, and encourage children to read along until they are able to read the story fluently.

Vocabulary

Using a Dictionary

Divide the class into small groups, and assign each group a word or two from the story, such as *victory*, *fiesta*, *sombreros*, *mariachi*, *piñata*, and *tortillas*. Invite children to use a dictionary to find the definitions. Have children write the definition for their word(s) and read them to the class. Ask the small groups to write at least two sentences for each word, and have the groups share their sentences with the class.

Comprehension

Understanding Descriptive Writing

Ask children what senses the author used to describe the Cinco de Mayo celebration. Encourage children to reread the story and circle each word (i.e., *sights, sounds, smells, tastes*). Ask children *Did the story remind you of a place you have been or something you have done before? How? Did the sights, sounds, smells, and tastes the author described help you feel like you were at the fiesta? Why?*

Exciting Celebration!

SKILL: IDENTIFYING EXCLAMATORY SENTENCES

Materials
- Celebrating Cinco de Mayo: Fiesta Time! reproducible (page 81)
- bookbinding materials

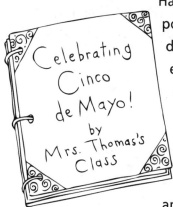

Have children find and circle all of the exclamation points on their reproducible story, and tell children to read aloud those sentences with expression. Ask children to compare the expression in the sentences with statements from the story that end with a period. Invite children to use information from the story or their own knowledge of Cinco de Mayo to write three sentences that each end with an exclamation point. Encourage children to illustrate their sentences, and bind their work in a class book titled "Celebrating Cinco de Mayo!"

Sensory Stroll

SKILL: ORGANIZING INFORMATION

Materials
- Sensory Stroll reproducible (page 85)
- scissors
- glue

Make a class set of the Sensory Stroll reproducible. Place the pages at a center with scissors and glue. Explain to children why it is important to organize information from a story (e.g., it helps us understand better; we see and remember details more clearly). Invite children to cut apart the boxes at the bottom of the Sensory Stroll reproducible. Ask children to arrange each word under the sensory heading where it was mentioned in the story. Caution children that some words may seem to fit in more than one category (e.g., you can taste *and* smell beans), so encourage them to reread the story to look up the correct answers. Have children glue the words in place after they have checked their work.

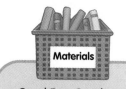

Fiesta Food

SKILL: GRAPHING

Copy a class set of the Good Eats Graph reproducible. Ask children to name five Mexican foods they like to eat. Write their answers on the board. Give each child a copy of the Good Eats Graph reproducible. Ask children to write the name of each food in the "Favorite Foods" boxes at the bottom of the columns on their reproducible. Have children vote on their favorite food. Ask children to raise their hand high when you call out their favorite Mexican food, and remind children that they can only vote one time. Write the results on the board. Help children use the data shown on the board to color in the appropriate spaces on their graph. Have students answer on the back of their reproducible the following questions: *What is the most popular food on the graph? What is the least popular food on the graph? How many people voted for _____ and _____? How many more people like _____ than _____?*

Fluffy Flags

SKILL: DEVELOPING FINE MOTOR SKILLS

Copy a class set of The Flag of Mexico reproducible on white construction paper. Place the pages at a center along with the other materials. Tell children to color the eagle on the Mexican flag brown and the leaves green. Show children how to cut tissue paper into 2-inch (5 cm) squares. Show children how to place the eraser end of a pencil in the center of a green square and twist it. Tell children to dip the paper in glue and then attach it to the left side of the flag. Have children continue until the block on the left is covered with green tissue paper. Ask children to cover the block on the right with red tissue paper, using the same technique.

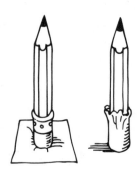

Name: _____

Sensory Stroll

The Sights of Cinco de Mayo	The Sounds of Cinco de Mayo
The Smells of Cinco de Mayo	The Tastes of Cinco de Mayo

colorful dresses	tortillas	tacos
dancers	singing	sombreros
children cheer	rice	beans
enchiladas	sweet treats	mariachi band

Name: _____

Good Eats Graph

10					
9					
8					
7					
6					
5					
4					
3					
2					
1					

Number of Students

Favorite Foods

(green)

(red)

It's almost Mother's Day.
I want to show my mom I love her in a
    special way.

I'll paint a little box.

I'll put in a teddy bear.
It shows how we love to bear hug.

I'll put in a piece of gum.
It shows how we always stick together.

I'll put in some nuts.
They show how silly we like to be.

I'll put in a bandage.
It shows how she always comes
    to my rescue.

I'll put in a chocolate kiss.
It shows how good it feels to be loved.

And, Mom, don't forget . . .
I'll love you forever!

Instant Lessons

Phonemic Awareness

Phoneme Deletion and Addition

Invite children to follow along as you read aloud the reproducible story. Tell children to point to *stick* on their reproducible story. Ask *If we take the /s/ off of* **stick**, *what word is left?* (i.e., *tick*). Name other words from the text (e.g., *shows, stick, put, in, hand*), and tell children to delete or add a sound to make a new word.

Phonics

Long *a*: *-ay, -ai, -ey*

Write *-ay, -ai,* and *-ey* on the board. Divide the class into small groups, and ask them to highlight on their reproducible the words that contain these long *a* spelling patterns. Assign one long *a* word from the text (e.g., *day* or *paint*) to each group, and invite them to make a list of other words with the same vowel pattern pronounced the same way (e.g., *clay* or *rain*). Ask a volunteer from each group to read aloud their list.

Fluency

Partner Reading

Read aloud the reproducible story several times. Then pair together children of similar reading levels, and invite them to take turns reading the text to each other until they can read it fluently.

Vocabulary

Adding Suffixes

Invite children to find and circle *love* on their reproducible story. Ask them to find another word with *love* in it (e.g., *loved*). Explain how adding a suffix slightly changes the meaning of the word. Write *-s, -ed,* and *-ing* on the board, and ask children to add these suffixes to *love*. Have children brainstorm a sentence for each new word. Then write *paint, show,* and *hug* on the board. Ask children to find these words on their reproducible story and circle them. Tell children to add the suffixes to each of the words and then write sentences for them.

Comprehension

Beginning/End/Middle Summarizing

Ask children to tell you what is happening at the beginning of the story (i.e., the bear is making a memory box), and write their ideas at the top of the board. Ask children to tell you the last thing that happened in the story (i.e., the bear gives her mom the box and says "I love you"). Write that information at the bottom of the board. Have children give you only the most important information to tie the beginning and ending together (i.e., she puts items in the box that remind her of her mom), and write that information in the middle of the board. Read aloud the summary together.

Flowers for Mom

SKILL: USING CONTRACTIONS

Copy and color the Contraction Cards, Mom's Flowers, and Contraction Flowers reproducible pages. Cut apart the Contraction Cards and Contraction Flowers. For a self-checking feature, write on the back of each Contraction Card the two words that make up the contraction. Place the prepared materials at a center, and arrange the Contraction Cards in a pile. Invite children to draw the top card, read the contraction, and place the card on the dress of the "mom" cutout. Ask children to find the two Contraction Flowers with the words that make up the contraction. Have children "give" the Contraction Flowers to the mom by placing them on her hands. Encourage children to check their work before moving on to the next Contraction Card.

Materials

- Contraction Cards reproducible (page 92)
- Mom's Flowers reproducible (page 93)
- Contraction Flowers reproducible (page 94)
- crayons or markers
- scissors

My Mom Is the Best

SKILL: COMPLETING SENTENCES

Materials

- About Mom reproducible (page 95)

Copy a class set of the About Mom reproducible, and read the sentences with children. Encourage them to think carefully before completing each sentence in their best handwriting. The reproducible can be glued to the back of their Marvelous Mom artwork (see page 91) and presented as a Mother's Day gift.

Mom's Memory Box

SKILL: ESTIMATING AND SORTING

Materials

Copy a class set of the Memory Box Estimation reproducible. Place the gummy bears, gum, peanuts, bandages, and chocolate kisses in a box; and write *Mom's Memory Box* on one side. Write *Bears*, *Gum*, *Peanuts*, *Bandages*, and *Kisses* on separate containers. Place the reproducible pages, box, and containers at a center. Invite children to open the box and estimate how many items they see altogether. Ask children to record their estimation on the chart. Then have children sort the items without counting them. Ask children to estimate the number of each item and record their individual estimations on their chart. Finally, have children count the items and write the numbers on their chart in the column labeled "Actual No. of Items."

- Memory Box Estimation reproducible (page 96)
- 10–50 each of gummy bears, pieces of gum, peanuts, bandages, chocolate kisses
- small box with a lid

Marvelous Mom

SKILLS: DEVELOPING FINE MOTOR SKILLS AND FOLLOWING DIRECTIONS

Materials

Make several copies of the Mother's Dress reproducible on card stock, and cut them out. Tell children to use the cutouts to trace a dress on the back of a piece of wallpaper. Have children cut out the dress and glue it to the center of a piece of white construction paper. Have children use crayons or markers to draw the head, arms, and legs for their "mom." Encourage them to glue yarn to the top of the head to make hair. To add interest, have children glue their completed About Mom reproducible (page 95) to the back of their Marvelous Mom art.

- Mother's Dress reproducible (page 97)
- card stock
- scissors
- wallpaper
- white construction paper
- glue
- crayons or markers
- yarn

Contraction Cards

it's	can't	won't	he'll
isn't	shouldn't	I'll	don't
she'll	we're	couldn't	haven't
aren't	they've	they'll	we'll
you're	you've	they're	we've

Mom's Flowers

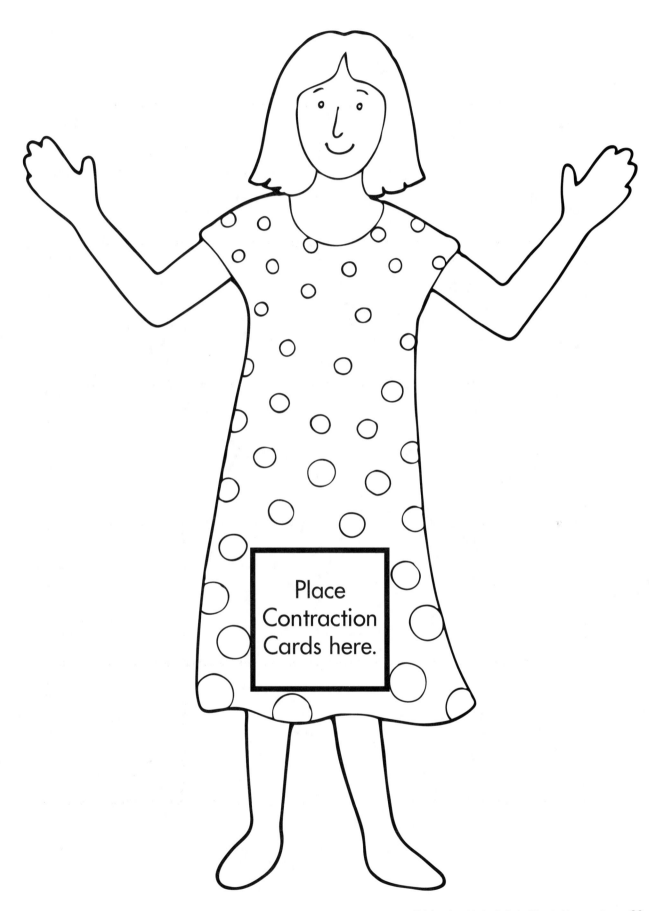

Place Contraction Cards here.

Contraction Flowers

it is I will

can not do she

he we are could

should have you they

Name: _____

About Mom

My mom is the best mom in the whole world because

_____

_____.

One thing my mom can do really well is

_____

_____.

It makes me laugh when my mom

_____

_____.

My mom can really cook _____,
but I'm not crazy about her _____.

My mom works very hard to _____.

I like it when my mom wears _____.

My favorite thing to do with my mom is

_____

_____.

I really love my mom because

_____

_____.

Memory Box Estimation

Items	Estimation	Actual No. of Items
All items in the box		
Bears		
Gum		
Peanuts		
Bandages		
Kisses		

Mother's Dress

Today we are going to make Father's Day cards.

I don't live with my dad.
I have a stepfather.
I don't have a dad.

You can make a card for any man you love and respect.

I'm making a card for my dad.
He taught me to ride a bike.

I'm making a card for my grandpa.
He reads me a story every night.

I'm making a card for my uncle.
He takes me to the park.

I'm making a card for my big brother.
He helps me with my homework.

I'm making a card for my stepfather.
He coaches my soccer team.

Father's Day isn't just for fathers.

Father's Day is for special people!

Instant Lessons

Phonemic Awareness

Phoneme Substitution

Read aloud the fifth sentence on the reproducible story, and emphasize the word *man*. Repeat the word. Say *If we take off the /n/ and replace it with /d/, what word do we have?* (i.e., *mad*). Change some sounds in other words from the text to make new words. For example, change the /n/ in *night* to /l/ to make *light*.

Phonics

Long Vowel Sounds

Write on index cards the words with long vowel sounds from the story (e.g., *today*, *day*, *make*, *takes*, *we*, *he*, *reads*). Give one index card to each child. Ask children to walk around the room and show each other their cards. Ask children to find others with words that have the same long vowel sound, and tell them to form a group. Invite individual groups to read their words and identify their long vowel sound.

Fluency

Choral Reading

Read aloud the story, and model fluent reading. Invite children to join you in reading aloud. Repeat at various times during the day or over the course of a week until children can read the story fluently on their own.

Vocabulary

Repeated Exposure

Explain to children that the class is going to have a "Respect Race." Ask children to print their name on an index card, and have them cut out circles from construction paper to glue to the bottom of the card to make a "car." Staple the cars in a column on the left side of a bulletin board, and make a finish line on the far right side. Have children use the word *respect* to write or dictate on another index card a sentence about a person. Staple the sentence cards beside children's cars. Tell children that each sentence card they write about someone helps their car reach the finish line.

Comprehension

Generating Questions

Brainstorm with children a list of questions from the story; write the questions on the board, but do not answer them. Ask a child who thinks he or she knows the story well to volunteer to answer a question. Invite another child to choose the question to ask the volunteer. If the volunteer answers the question correctly, invite someone else to ask the volunteer another question. If the volunteer does not know the answer, invite another child to help answer the question. Choose another volunteer, and repeat the activity.

Tidy Ties

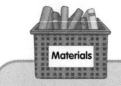

SKILLS: ARRANGING WORDS IN ALPHABETICAL ORDER AND WRITING SENTENCES

Materials

- Dad's Ties reproducible (page 102)
- scissors
- dictionary
- white or light-colored construction paper
- glue

Copy a class set of the Dad's Ties reproducible, and have children cut apart the "ties." Ask children to arrange the ties in alphabetical order on their desks, and encourage children to use a dictionary for help if necessary. Without changing the order of the words, challenge children to write on construction paper six sentences, each containing two Dad's Ties words. Have children glue the tie cutouts in place of the words. For example, a child's first sentence may read *Dad, **are** you going to put my **bike** together?*

Perfect Papas

SKILL: COMPLETING SENTENCES

Materials

- Man-of-the-Year Award reproducible (page 103)

Copy a class set of the Man-of-the-Year Award reproducible. Brainstorm with children what their dad or another male role model may do to deserve this award. Give each child a reproducible, and encourage children to complete the sentences about this person. Invite children to present their awards on Father's Day. Another option is to glue this completed paper to the back of the Pieces of Dad Collage (see page 101).

Daddy Digits

SKILL: UNDERSTANDING PLACE VALUES

Materials

- Valuable Dads reproducible (page 104)
- Number Cards reproducible (page 105)
- card stock
- crayons or markers
- scissors
- paper

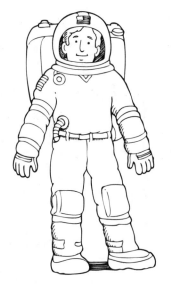

Copy a set of Valuable Dads and Number Cards reproducible pages on card stock. Color and cut them apart. For a self-checking feature, write the place value of the underlined number on the back of each Number Card. Place the pieces at a center. Review with children place values to the thousands. Ask children to look at the underlined number on each Number Card. Invite them to place the Number Card under the "dad" that names the place value of the underlined number. For example, a Number Card that reads 1,2<u>3</u>4 should be placed under the Tens Dad.

Pieces of Dad Collage

SKILL: VISUALIZING

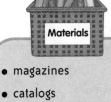

Materials

- magazines
- catalogs
- scissors
- glue
- construction paper
- crayons or markers

Encourage children to picture in their minds what their dad or other male role model looks like. Ask questions like *What color is his hair? What color are his eyes? Does he wear a suit to work, or does he dress casually? Is he tall? Does he have a particularly striking feature of any kind?* Invite children to look through the magazines and catalogs to find details of pictures that remind them of their dad. Have them use scissors to cut out only those pieces (e.g., a child whose father is bearded may cut out only the beard from a picture). Invite children to glue the pieces onto construction paper. Encourage children to draw the features they can't find examples for. To add interest, have children glue their completed Man-of-the-Year Award reproducible (page 103) to the back of the collage.

Dad's Ties

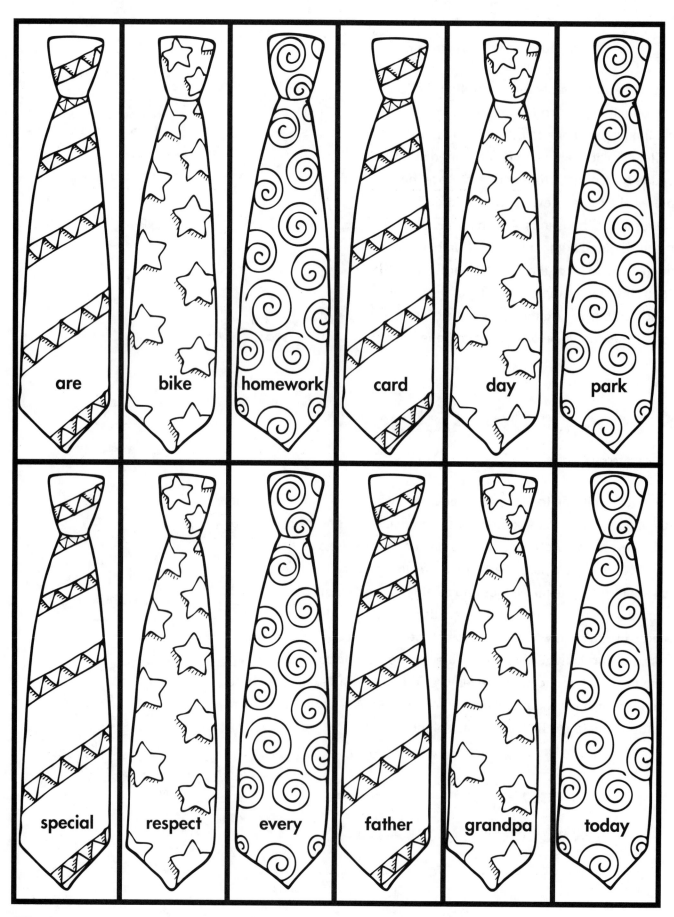

are

bike

homework

card

day

park

special

respect

every

father

grandpa

today

Name: _____

 **Man-of-the-Year Award**

Presented to: _____

You deserve the Man-of-the-Year Award because

_____

_____ .

One thing you do really well is

_____

_____ .

It makes me laugh when you

_____

_____ .

You can really _____ , but

_____ is not your strong suit.

You work very hard to _____ .

I like it when you _____ .

My favorite thing to do with you is

_____

_____ .

I really love you because you

_____

_____ .

Valuable Dads

Number Cards

156<u>6</u>	<u>6</u>32	<u>4</u>6	890<u>5</u>
<u>7</u>2	<u>3</u>869	2<u>9</u>46	5<u>8</u>
<u>4</u>82	20<u>5</u>7	<u>9</u>572	<u>9</u>54
<u>9</u>	<u>2</u>661	<u>9</u>5	<u>4</u>321

All year round, I show that I am proud to live in America.

Labor Day is a time I honor hardworking Americans.
Labor Day also reminds me that a new school year is about to begin!

Veterans Day is a time I honor soldiers who fought for America.
Veteran's Day is on the eleventh day of the eleventh month—November 11!

Memorial Day is a time I honor people who made America great!
Memorial Day also reminds me that it is time for summer vacation!

Flag Day is a time I honor our flag, the Stars and Stripes.
Flag Day is on June 14, right at the start of summer.

My favorite American holiday comes right in the middle of summer.
We have parades and picnics.
We celebrate freedom.
We watch fireworks at night.
We remember that America became a nation in 1776.

Can you guess which American holiday is my favorite?
Independence Day, the 4th of July!
Let's celebrate freedom for America!

I celebrate America all year round.
I'm proud to live in America!

Instant Lessons

Phonemic Awareness

Phoneme Substitution

Read aloud the first line from the reproducible story, and emphasize the word *that*. Say *If we take off the /th/ and replace it with /h/, what word do we have?* (i.e., *hat*). Change sounds in other words from the text to make new words. For example, change the /i/ in *in* to /o/ to make *on,* or change the /d/ in *day* to /p/ to make *pay.*

Phonics

The Schwa Sound

Read aloud the story, and emphasize the schwa sound (i.e., the unstressed neutral vowel, as /a/ in *sofa*) in the words *America, about, Veterans, Memorial, celebrate, freedom,* and *nation.* Repeat words containing the schwa sound until children can identify the sound. Reread the story, and write on the board the words with the schwa sound. Invite children to underline the letters on their reproducible story that represent the schwa sound.

Fluency

Choral Reading

Read aloud the story to model fluent reading. Then, at various times during the day or over the course of a week, invite children to read along with you until they, too, can read the story fluently.

Vocabulary

Using a Dictionary

Read aloud the story, and invite children to follow along with their eyes. Tell children to underline *patriotic, honor, freedom,* and *nation* when they appear in the text, and write them on the board. Ask children to look up the words in the dictionary and read aloud the definitions to the class. Encourage children to look through textbooks and picture books to find images they think illustrate the meaning of each word.

Comprehension

Using a Semantic Web

Draw on the board a web with a circle in the center and five circles surrounding it. Write *American Patriotic Holidays* in the center circle. Invite children to name the five holidays mentioned in the book, and write one holiday in each circle in the web. Ask children to look on their reproducible story for information about each holiday and to write the information beside the corresponding circles.

Honoring Homophones

SKILL: RECOGNIZING HOMOPHONES

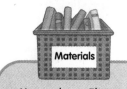

Materials

- Homophone Flags reproducible (page 110)
- scissors
- glue
- crayons or markers

Copy a class set of the Homophone Flags reproducible. Explain to children that a homophone is a word that sounds the same as another word but has a different meaning and possibly a different spelling. Give each child a Homophone

made

My mom _____ a good lunch for me today.

Flags reproducible, and ask him or her to cut apart the Star Fields at the bottom of the page. Have children read the words in the Star Fields and the sentences on the Homophone Flags. Explain that they need to match the word in the Star Fields to the sentence that it completes. Ask children to glue the appropriate Star Fields word in the top left corner of the Homophone Flag. When children are finished, have them color their paper.

Patriotic Paper

SKILL: PERSUASIVE WRITING

Materials

- Celebrating Patriotic Holidays: Honoring America reproducible (page 106)
- Patriotic Persuasion reproducible (page 111)

Copy a class set of the Patriotic Persuasion reproducible. Invite children to choose their favorite holiday from the story. Brainstorm with children all the reasons people celebrate the different holidays as well as people's feelings about the holidays. Tell children to pretend the President is thinking of canceling their chosen holiday. Ask children to write on their paper a letter to the President that explains why the holiday is important and why it must not be canceled.

Dear Mr. President,

American as Apple Pie

SKILL: GRAPHING

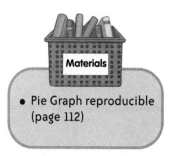

Copy a class set of the Pie Graph reproducible, and explain that a pie graph is one way to show different pieces of a whole group. Review with children the different holidays in the story. Take a vote of favorite patriotic holidays. Ask children to raise their hand high when you call their favorite holiday, and remind them they can only vote once. Record the results on the board, and ask children to record the results at the bottom of their paper. Then work with students to assign a large or small area of the pie graph to each holiday, based on the number of votes it received.

High-Flying Flags

SKILLS: DEVELOPING FINE MOTOR SKILLS AND FOLLOWING DIRECTIONS

Cut pieces of blue construction paper into four equal rectangles. Place all materials at a center. Pour red and white paint into separate trays. Give each child a piece of white construction paper, and have him or her place it lengthwise on the desk. Invite children to glue a blue rectangle to the top left corner of their white paper. Have children dip a star sponge into white paint and use it to stamp several stars on the blue square. Show children how to dip the edge of a piece of cardboard into the red paint and use it to stamp seven stripes beside and below the blue square to complete their flag.

- scissors
- 9" x 12" (23 cm x 30.5 cm) construction paper (blue and white)
- paint (red and white)
- trays
- glue
- small star-shaped sponge
- cardboard

Homophone Flags

My mom _____ a good lunch for me today.

I like to count the stars at _____.

The _____ cleaned the house from top to bottom.

The _____ rode his horse toward the castle.

I will _____ a letter to my pen pal.

I have a left and a _____ hand.

Star Fields

knight	right	write	maid	night	made

Name: _____

Patriotic Persuasion

_____

_____

_____

_____

_____

_____

_____

_____

_____

_____

_____

_____

_____

Pie Graph

_____ children in our class like Labor Day best.

_____ children in our class say Veterans Day is very special.

_____ children in our class love Memorial Day most.

_____ children in our class feel that Flag Day is fine.

_____ children in our class think Independence Day is awesome.